VROMAN'S
PASADENA

P9-DXN-824

Projets des Avenües
de la Ville.

Plaine de
St Michel.

Les Minimes.

Place d'Irmes.

P.N.D.
du mont.

N.D.
du mont.

P. de N.D. de
la Garde.

P. de Rome.

Nouvelles Fortifications.

BOOKS BY M. F. K. FISHER

A CONSIDERABLE TOWN

A
Considerable
Town

M. F. K. FISHER

Alfred A. Knopf

NEW YORK

1978

This is a Borzoi Book
Published by Alfred A. Knopf, Inc.

Copyright © 1964, 1977, 1978 by M. F. K. Fisher
All rights reserved under International and
Pan-American Copyright Conventions.
Published in the United States by Alfred A. Knopf, Inc.,
New York, and simultaneously in Canada by Random House
of Canada Limited, Toronto. Distributed by Random House,
Inc., New York.

Part of Chapter 2 appeared in the
Travel Section of *The New York Times*
on December 18, 1977.
Part of Chapter 7 appeared in
Gourmet Magazine, May 1978.
Part II of Chapter 11 was originally published as
"The Mahogony Tree" in *Woman's Day*.
Reprinted by permission of *Woman's Day* Magazine, a
Fawcett publication.

Library of Congress Cataloging in Publication Data
Fisher, Mary Frances Kennedy, 1908-
A considerable town.

1. Marseille—Description.   2. Fisher, Mary
Frances Kennedy, 1908-   I. Title.
DC801.M37F57   1978   944'.91   77-20369
ISBN 0-394-42711-4

Manufactured in the United States of America
Published May 1, 1978
Reprinted Twice
Fourth Printing, August 1978

For my girls and my sister

MARSEILLE: 13 B. du Rh., Provence; 893 771 h.

Voir: Basilique N.D. de-la-Garde; La Canebière; Vieux Port; Corniche Président J. F. Kennedy; Port moderne; Palais Longchamps; Basilique St.-Victor; Cathédrale de la Major et anc. Cathédrale de la Major; Parc du Pharo.

Musees: 4

Excursions: Bateau, autobus, chemin de fer, avion (Office de Tourisme, Acceuil de France, T.C.F., etc.)

Paris 777 km, Lyons 315, Nice 187, Toulon 64, Toulouse 400, Turin 370

Hotels: 28, de 'grand luxe' à 'simple mais convenable'

Restaurants agréables: 20 en ville, 5 sur la Corniche

—1976 Michelin Guide to *France*

MARSEILLE: Bouches du Rhone, Provence: postal zone, 13

To see: Basilica of Notre Dame de la Garde; The Canebière; Old Port; Cliff-highway J. F. Kennedy; Modern Port; Longchamps Palace; Basilica of St.-Victor; Cathedral of La Major and ancient Cathedral; the Pharo Park.

Museums: four main ones listed.

Transportation and **Excursions** by water, railway, bus, and air. **Information:** Tourism Office, French Welcome Center, etc.

Paris, 777 km. from Marseille; Lyons, 315; Nice, 187; Toulon, 64; Toulouse, 400; Turin, 370.

Hotels: 28 listed, ranging from luxurious to "plain but decent."

Restaurants: in the same categories, 20 listed in the city, and 5 on the Kennedy Corniche.

—A simplified version of the several pages devoted to Marseille in the 1976 Michelin Guide to *France*

ICI
VERS L'AN 600 AVANT J.C.
DES MARINS GRECS ONT ABORDES
VENANT DE PHOCEE
ILS FONDERENT MARSEILLE
D'OU RAYONNA EN OCCIDENT
LA CIVILISATION

[Here,
in about 600 B.C.,
Greek sailors of Phocea came ashore.
They founded Marseille,
from which civilization spread
throughout the
Western world.]

—Bronze plate sunk in pavement of
the Quai des Belges on the Vieux Port,
at the foot of the Canebière

Alphonse de Lamartine   en 1832
Frédéric Chopin   en 1839
George Sand
    séjournèrent en cet hôtel

[Lamartine,
and Chopin with George Sand,
stayed in this hotel]

—Plaque outside the entrance of
the Hotel Beauvau

∨

PLAN
DE
MARSEILLE
Ville considérable de Provence
Fameux Port sur la Mer Méditerranée
par
Nicolas de Fer
Graveur et Géographe
1702

[Map of Marseille,
a considerable town of Provence
and famous Mediterranean port . . . by Nicolas de Fer,
engraver and geographer,
1702]

CONTENTS

A CONSIDERABLE TOWN

Chapter I

THE PLACE
WHERE
I LOOKED

One of the many tantalizing things about Marseille is that most people who describe it, whether or not they know much about either the place or the languages they are supposedly using, write the same things. For centuries this has been so, and a typically modern opinion could have been given in 1550 as well as 1977.

Not long ago I read one, mercifully unsigned, in a San Francisco paper. It was full of logistical errors, faulty syntax, misspelled French words, but it hewed true to the familiar line that Marseille is doing its best to live up to a legendary reputation as world capital for "dope, whores, and street violence." It then went on to discuss, often erroneously, the essential ingredients of a true bouillabaisse! The familiar pitch had been made, and idle readers dreaming of a great seaport dedicated to heroin, prostitution, and rioting could easily skip the clumsy details of marketing for fresh fish. . . .

"Feature articles" like this one make it seem probable that many big newspapers, especially in English-reading countries, keep a few such mild shockers on hand in a back drawer, in case a few columns need filling on a rainy Sunday. Apparently people like to glance one more time at the same old words: evil, filthy, dangerous.

Sometimes such journalese is almost worth reading for its precociously obsolete views of a society too easy to forget. In 1929, for instance, shortly before the Wall Street Crash, a popular travel writer named Basil Woon published *A Guide to the Gay World of France: From Deauville to Monte Carlo* (Horace Liveright, New York). (By now even his use of word "gay" is quaintly naïve enough for a small chuckle. . . .)

Of course Mr. Woon was most interested in the Côte d'Azur, in those far days teeming and staggering with rich English and even richer Americans, but while he could not actively recommend staying in Marseille, he did remain true to his journalistic background with an expectedly titillating mention of it:

> If you are interested in how the other side of the world lives, a trip through old Marseilles—by daylight—cannot fail to thrill, but it is not wise to venture into this district at night unless dressed like a stevedore and well armed. Thieves, cutthroats, and other undesirables throng the narrow alleys, and sisters of scarlet sit in the doorways of their places of business, catching you by the sleeve as you pass by. The dregs of the world are here, unsifted. It is Port Said, Shanghai, Barcelona, and Sidney combined. Now that San Francisco has reformed, Marseilles is the world's wickedest port.

(Mr. Woon's last sentence, written some fifty years ago, is more provocative today than it was then, to anyone interested in the shifting politics of the West Coast of America. . . .)

While I either accept or deplore what other people report about the French town, and even feel that I understand why they are obliged to use the words they do (Give the public what it wants, etc., etc. . . .), I myself have a different definition of the place, which is as indefinable as Marseille itself: *Insolite*.

There seems to be no proper twin for this word in English; one simply has to sense or feel what it means. Larousse says that it is somewhat like "contrary to what is usual and normal." Dictionaries such as the Shorter Oxford and Webster's Third International try words like *apart, unique, unusual*. This is not enough, though . . . not quite right. Inwardly I know that it means *mysterious, unknowable*, and in plain fact, *indefinable*.

And that is Marseille: indefinable, and therefore *insolite*. And the strange word is as good as any to explain why the place haunts me and draws me, with its phoenixlike vitality, its implacably realistic beauty and brutality. The formula is plain: Marseille = *insolite*, therefore *insolite* = Marseille.

This semantical conclusion on my part may sound quibbling, but it seems to help me try to explain what connection there could possibly, logically, be between the town and me . . . why I have returned there for so long: a night, ten nights, many weeks or months.

Of course it is necessary to recognize that there is a special karma about Marseille, a karmic force that is mostly translated as wicked, to be avoided by all clean and righteous people. Travellers have long been advised to shun it like the pesthole it has occasionally been, or at best to stay there as short a time as possible before their next ship sets sail.

A true karmic force is supposed to build up its strength through centuries of both evil and good, in order to prevent

its transmigration into another and lesser form, and this may
well explain why Marseille has always risen anew from the
ashes of history. There seems to be no possible way to stamp
it out. Julius Caesar tried to, and for a time felt almost sure
that he had succeeded. Calamities caused by man's folly and
the gods' wrath, from the plagues ending in 1720 to the in-
vasions ending in the 1940s, have piled it with rotting bodies
and blasted rubble, and the place has blanched and staggered,
and then risen again. It has survived every kind of weapon
known to European warfare, from the ax and arrow to sophisticated derivatives of old Chinese gunpowder, and it is
hard not to surmise that if a nuclear blast finally leveled the
place, some short dark-browed men and women might even-
tually emerge from a few deep places, to breed in the salt
marshes that would gradually have revivified the dead waters
around the Old Port. . . .

Meanwhile, Marseille lives, with a unique strength that
plainly scares less virile breeds. Its people are proud of being
"apart," and critics mock them for trying to sound even more
Italianate than they are, trying to play roles for the tourists:
fishermen ape Marcel Pagnol's *Marius* robustly; every fish-
wife is her own Honorine. The Pinball Boys are thinner and
more viperous there than anywhere in Europe, they assume as
true Marseillais, and the tarts are tarter and the old hags
older and more haggish than anywhere in the world. . . .

Behind this almost infantile enjoyment of playing their
parts on a superb stage with changing backdrops that are
certainly *insolite*, and a full orchestration of every sound
effect from the ringings of great bells to the whine of the
tramontane and the vicious howl of the mistral, held together
by sirens from ambulances and ships, and the pinpricks of
complaining seagulls . . . behind this endlessly entertaining

and absorbing melodrama, a secret life-source provides its inner nourishment to the citizens.

There is a strong religious blood flowing in that corporate body. Catholics and other Christians, Communists, Free-thinkers, Arabs, Gypsies, all admit to an acceptance of powers beyond their questionings, whether or not they admit to *being* "believers." The gigantic bell Marie-Joséphine, at the top of Notre Dame de la Garde, rings for every soul that has ever lived there, no matter how much a race-bound parishioner of St. Victor might deny the right of a Moslem in the Panier across the Old Port to understand its reassuring voice.

Naturally, in a place as old and *insolite* as Marseille, there is a strong dependence on forces that are loosely called occult, or mystical, or perhaps demonic. There are many fortune-tellers, usually thriving in their chosen ways of neighborhood help or prestigious social acclaim. The best known of the Tarot cards were adapted to a special ritual that evolved there, and are called by the town's name. Cabalistic signs are often in or on graffiti, political or otherwise, and it is plain that the right people will see and understand them. Why not? After all, the churches build their altars over early Christian sepulchers laid in turn upon the stones of temples built to Artemis and Adonis, who in turn . . .

There is a good description of the withdrawn side of the noisy, rough-talking Marseillais in one of Simenon's books about Inspector Maigret. It was written about another French town, but it is Marseille to me:

> . . . a stone jungle, where you can disappear for months; where often you do not hear of a crime until weeks after it has been committed; where thousands of human beings . . . live on the fringes of the Law, in a world where they can find as many accomplices and hideouts as they need, and

where the police put out their bait now and then and pull in a fish they were waiting for, all the while depending more for such luck on a telephone call from a jealous girl or an informer. . . .

This quasi-occult mutism is what has helped defeat the invaders of Marseille, I think. Certainly it baffled the last militant "occupants" in the 1940s. Many different stories are told about how and why a large part of the ancient Greco-Roman bank of the Old Port was destroyed by the Germans, but the basic reason for this move was probably that they simply could not keep track of what was going on in the deep warrens that went up from the Quai du Port past Les Accoules toward La Vieille Charité and the Place des Moulins. What was worse, they could not tell from the flat black eyes, the blank unmoved faces of occupants of this filthy old neighborhood, the pimps and bawds and small-time gangsters who went there as a natural refuge when their other ways of life were interrupted by war, which of them were working with what appointed or subterranean leaders, and even which of them might be town fathers in false beards rather than black marketeers dealing indirectly with the invaders.

The answer was to get rid of the whole infamous district, and it was easy to have the German-appointed city council approve a plan to blow up the mess from underground. It was done neatly, with complete evacuation of the helpless residents and full warning to the numberless unknown invisibles who were using the old tunnels for their special version of the Liberation. (Some other destruction during that dubious time was less circumspect, of course, and a few foul tricks were blamed on the invaders when an orphanage, or a clinic, say, was without notice shattered from above and not below ground. . . .)

Soon after the dirty tunnels and gutters above the Quai

du Port were mined and hopefully wiped out, they were once more in full swing, of course: rats and moles know how to dig again. A lot of the diggers were summarily lined up and shot, but that did not seem to impress the strange breed called Marseillais for so many centuries. Some thirty-five years later, the whole quarter is threatened with a new demolition, to make way for high-rise housing projects, but the people who live there, as elsewhere in the big town, remain impassive and tough and sardonic . . . that is to say, *insolite.*

This cannot be a guidebook, the kind that tells how, with a chart to be got free from the driver of the tour, to follow a green line from A to G and then switch to either the red or the yellow lines to Z, depending on how weary or hungry one may feel. I am not meant to tell anyone where to go in Marseille, nor even why I myself went where I did there, and saw and smelled and felt as I did. All I can do in this explanation about my being there is to write something about the town itself, through my own senses.

I first spent a night there in late 1929, and since then I have returned even oftener than seems reasonable. Beginning in 1940, there were wars, both worldwide and intramural, and then I managed to regain my old rhythm. Each time I went back, I felt younger: a chronological miracle, certainly!

One reason I now try to explain all this is that when I cannot return, for physical or perhaps financial reasons, I will stay so enriched and heartened by what I have known there that I should be the envy of every crowned head of several worlds. I boast, and rightly. Nobody who has lived as deeply for as long as I have in Marseille-Insolite can be anything but blessed.

There is an almost impossible lot of things to see there, and for one reason or another I know many of them, and have been part of them with people I loved (another proud boast!). If I started to tell why I wished everybody in the world could do the same, it would make a whole book, a personal guide tour, and that is not what I am meant to write, according to my secret directives. I would say words like Longchamps, Borély, Cantini, Les Accoules, St. Victor, St. Nicolas, La Place des Moulins, La Vieille Charité, Notre Dame de la Garde, La Rue de Rome . . . and it would be for every unexpected reason known to human beings, from the smell of a sick lion in a zoo behind Longchamps to an obviously necrophilic guardian of the tombs in Borély to the cut of an exquisite tweed skirt in a Paris boutique on the Rome. Each reason I gave for wanting some people to know why I've been there would make the guide a long hymn, hopefully shot through with practical asides about how far Borély is from town, and how steep the walk is up through the Panier to the Vieille Charité, and how much to tip the elderly patient men at places like the Musée des Docks Romains . . . and yes, why did I not mention it before? Other places, other sounds: they tumble in my head like pebbles under a waterfall, and all I know is that I must try to understand why I myself go back to this strange beautiful town.

If I could be in only one part of it, I would go directly to the Old Port, and stay there. I know that a lot of people consider it hopelessly touristic or noisy or vulgar. I feel at ease there, perhaps more so than in any other populous place I have ever known. Most of the reasons for this escape me or were never even guessed, but the fact remains that if I could within the next three minutes go by teleportation to the Quai des Belges on the Vieux Port, I would know exactly what to do and say and eat, and would feel as welcome as any shadow. It is very nice to feel like this.

The Vieux Port has a narrow entrance, past the Pharo Palace that Napoleon III built for his Empress, so that from almost any part of its three quays it looks landlocked. Every Marseillais, though, and almost every stranger there, knows that out through the tumultuous inlet and past the jetties of the new port of La Joliette lie several little bleak harsh islands, one of them crowned with the tomblike Château d'If that Dumas peopled with his noble ghosts.

Coming back from the Château, sometimes a very rough trip indeed, the Rive Neuve is on one's right, with the Abbey of St. Victor and then La Garde towering over it, and on the waterfront the façade of the Criée, the public auction house for fish. It looks something like a fragment of the Gare de Lyon in Paris, tall and with grimed glassy walls. It is said to be doomed, now that so much transportation is done by trucks and rail from all over Europe, with their mounting traffic problems, but I first heard this as an imminent fact some ten years ago, and it still hums and screams from late night until predawn, and then is as quiet as a church, except for the men who hose down the walls and trestle tables and floors for the next night's biddings. There are usually a few trawlers docked alongside to unload big catches or wait for cleanups.

The Rive Neuve is patchy and beautiful, architecturally, with some fine blocks of buildings that went up at the town end of the Port after the galleys stopped being built in the middle of the eighteenth century, a surprisingly short time ago. There is a dwindling number of good restaurants either on or just off the Quai, and the little fishhouses tacked onto the massive old blocks are tacky indeed to look at, and mostly evanescent. Portside there are private moorings for pleasure boats and larger yachts, a couple of clubs, generous moorings for small professional fishing boats. The feeling is lively, expert, no-nonsense, with several little cafés and chandleries and so on across the Quai.

Auto traffic is heavy and fast there, because of the cars that tear through the tunnel under the mouth of the Old Port from inland. Until the late 1940s, that end of the Port was hurdled by a strange thin loop of steel, referred to locally by several names, the most respectful being the "shore-to-shore hustler." Once Simenon wrote of it as a "gigantesque metal carcass, cutting across the horizon, on which one can make out, from a distance, tiny human beings." Raoul Dufy said it even better, with paint.

It seems odd to me that I never noticed the obtrusive "*pont transbordeur,*" until it was gone when I went back after the Occupation, in about 1951. It had always been there when I was, but since I had never seen the horizon any way but barred, I accepted it without question as part of the magic. It was no more gigantesque than any other man-made edifice: Notre Dame de la Garde, ugly but inspiring; St. Victor, ugly but reassuring; the aerial bridge, ugly but practical. Then when I returned to Marseille with my two small girls, I stood in a window in the old Hotel Beauvau on the Quai des Belges and felt a shock that made me gasp: the bridge was gone! The sky was free! Our eyes could look out over the boats, past the Pharo, which from the harbor always seemed more like a hospital than a palace, and then bend down as surely as any seagull's onto the tumble of rough water into La Joliette and our own Port! Perhaps it was the way a young sheep feels after its first shearing, very lightsome and cool suddenly.

The Quai des Belges is the shortest of the Port's three shores, at the head, the land end, of the little harbor. Like all centers of life past and present, it is concentrated, so that it has fine-to-sad restaurants and brasseries and commerce and mad traffic and a church and a bus terminal cramped onto the land side, with a subway station to open shortly, and then on the Port side docks for all the excursion boats to the Château d'If, and so on, with careful room for the fishermen to chug in six or seven mornings a week to set up their rickety tables in the casual market that strings out along the wide sidewalk.

For a long time in my Marseille life, the Quai des Belges had a sloping place where boats could be drawn up onto the pavement. When the wind was wild, water came onto the street, over the big plaque that tells how the Phoceans landed there. Then in perhaps the early sixties, some time after the *pont transbordeur* was taken down, the sloping pebbly pavement was made level with the rest of the Quai, and the edge went sharply down into the water so that it was uniformly convenient for the fishermen to put in with their catches for their wives to sell. Who dragged his craft up on shore, anymore, for a rest or some quick repairs? What fine ladies waited there to be rowed into mid-Port and then handed up to their sailing vessels?

One time, before the old beaching place was changed, I watched a small grey vessel of the American Navy swing delicately down the middle of the harbor, ease itself sideways within a few feet of the slope, and unload . . . disgorge . . . explode . . . what seemed like hundreds of sailors. I stood upstairs in my window, on that Christmas Eve, and it looked as if the young men flew onto the wet sloping pavement from their deck, without even touching the little boat alongside that was meant as a bridge. They gathered in knots on the windy Quai, and then melted fast in three directions, but mostly up the Can o' Beer.

Later a few strings of Christmas lights went on, looking pretty, but the next day there was almost no sign of life on the grim little vessel, and before the second dawn she slipped out of the harbor, presumably with her full crew. She was the last overtly military vessel I ever saw in the Vieux Port, although I suspect derring-do of international proportions in a few superpowerful-elegant-sleek-rich yachts I have watched there. (The whole district is more James Bond than Henry Kissinger!)

Around the north corner of the Quai des Belges, past the old church that is sinking slowly into the mouth of the Lacydon River (poetic justice, some infidels say!), the church that still shelters a few of the last of Marseille's infamous army of public beggars, there is the long ancient unequivocal stretch of wide street and wider portside pavement called the Quai du Port. Boats stretch from the Quai des Belges out to the Harbor Master's Quarters just before the Fort St. Jean and the entrance to the harbor. Near town they are small plain craft with oars, outboard motors and no masts, often scruffy, but looking as familiar as housecats. Until a few years ago, retired fishermen used to wait there to snag visitors, and take them jerking and bouncing on "tours" of La Joliette.

These self-styled tours were never the same, never dull. There were two or three little boats with awnings, I remember. They cost more, but were reassuring to visiting friends when we went over the bumps between the Vieux Port and the breakwater of the new port. One time in La Joliette we were putt-putting along under the prows of gigantic ships loading for Africa and Indo-China, and suddenly looked up into a beautiful Spanish or Italian vessel and its elegant Captain's Quarters, with mullioned windows and rich brocade curtains! It was a facsimile of one of Christopher Columbus's little toys, that had been made for movies and international fairs, and was being taken under motor power to Naples or Barcelona or some such coincidental port. The clean brutal outlines of a diesel freighter to Djakarta were almost a relief.

Farther along the Quai du Port, and especially in front of the little Town Hall that was saved from explosion by mutual agreement with the Invaders in 1943, there are dreamily beautiful yachts of every club and country. They come in and out. Usually they are in fine condition, at least to the eye, and now and then a lithe crewman polishes brass, but in general they are empty when we loiterers glance or stare at them. One time a "tall ship" with three masts, all painted a dull coal black, lay alongside the Town Hall for several weeks, and nobody seemed to know why, or what it was. It flew the French flag. And once in 1976 the ugliest hull I ever saw lay there, not attracting much notice.

It had faky anchors painted here and there near its prow, and was plainly some sort of mockery of everything beautiful about an ocean-going vessel, with almost no superstructure and yet without a single porthole that could be seen. It too was a flat ugly black, and was lettered minutely, *Club Méditerranée.* I knew about that so-called social corporation, of course, and asked a couple of Quai-watchers if it was going to be turned into a party ship. There was no answer, more than a shrug. It seemed strange, to look over from the Beauvau, too, and see that uncouth thing in front of the dainty little Town Hall.

Within a day or so, of course, when I was back in Aix and reading local interpretations of Marseille news instead of being there to garner the real truth of such matters (!), I learned that the ship was already famous, and would compete for the Atlantic International Cup on a solo voiage. It would be piloted mostly by electronics, and by a single Marseillais, alone in that dreadful carcass. I felt sick and fascinated and strangely embarrassed at my own unawareness, and I followed the log of the *Club Med* the whole way, and felt triumphant when it joined the "tall ships" in the great bicentennial parade on the Hudson River, July 4, 1976. I felt proud.

On the harbor water, which is somewhat cleaner as one goes along the Quai seaward, are docked the trawlers, the *chalutiers*, the vessels needing a deep draft for their enormous nets and, in port, their full hulls. They come into port to discharge their big fish across the harbor at the Criée, and then dock at the Quai du Port to keep their papers in order with the Harbor Master, and perhaps rest a few hours or days for the sakes of their crews. Drydocks mean going up the coast, although the smaller crafts have their own simple lifts along the Quai.

Most of the organizations of Vieux boat owners, professional and social, are housed portside on the ancient shore, and they are called Nautical Societies or Syndicates or Friendly Rowing Clubs or Lacydonian Brotherhoods or suchlike. They have simple clubhouses, firmly fenced off from the wide walk where people stroll and where nets are mended. Usually on weekends young couples chip at a small dangling hull, or paint seriously while the family dog or baby watches from the cobbles. Now and then a Sunday crowd on the Quai looks amiably over the fence as a group of amateur fishermen grill their catch of sardines and cool their fingers on plentiful bottles. The whole thing smells good: fish, wine, smoke from the burning driftwood; fresh paint from the next Société des Canotiers to the east; westward a whiff of tar from a modest drydock. On weekdays professionals take over the Quai, and watchers are fewer as men work hard on their boats or nets, and the air can be very salty.

Landside there are somber arcades almost hysterically lighted by countless thin deep espresso joints, and a few excellent restaurants that in fine weather flood their tables as far as possible out across the sidewalks toward the traffic, which is not quite as lethal as on the Rive Neuve. There seems no need for music, although now and then in summer a flameblower or a tumbler will pick up a few coins from the more sated diners.

As one moves back toward the Quai des Belges along the port, the gastronomy swings from pasta to bouillabaisse, and from Chianti to white house-wine, and the restaurants are more filled with tourists and with locals on a little weekend spree than they are with vacationing decorators and actors from "up North." It is pleasant, a good way to eat and talk, and behind, the pinball machines throb on, and the tiny espresso cups sit half-empty everywhere in the long bright bars.

And then behind the arcades and the pinball joints rise the graceful hills, where the Greeks and then the Romans built temples and theatres on the sites of older altars. Now the clock tower of Les Accoules rises sturdily, if off-time, as it did for other purposes in the thirteenth century, and leads up to the old Place des Moulins through streets that are cleaner than they have sometimes been, but still suspect to tidy travellers and even some City Fathers, who would like to get rid of them for high-rise condominiums.

And at the land's-end of the Port, high and straight behind the Quai des Belges to the west, new but lightsomely majestic, rises Longchamps, which cannot be suspected except from hilltops or out at sea. It is an astonishing public building, one that could never have been erected in France except in the mid-nineteenth century, when Napoleon III's taste was rampant. It spouts water in controlled extravagance from great carved mouths, down many churning basins toward the thirsty town, and on out along the course of the ancient Lacydon toward the open sea. It sweeps the Vieux Port cleaner than it has been since men started to pollute it some two thousand years ago, and then clogged it foully when they built over the mouth of the old river. Around this majestic waterworks that spews its blessings from the wicked river of the Durance, first curbed in 1838, is built a garishly wonderful palace that houses natural and manmade history, and that hides a relatively tiny little botanical garden and zoo. It is all almost nightmarish at close range, like being lost in a fetal Disneyland, but from afar, Longchamps is beautiful.

It is one of the reasons I want to say why I must return to its town. When I have tried to tell natives that I need to write about it, they are courteous in their own sardonic way. They do not mock too openly, but they manage to imply flatly that I am presumptuous: "Ah? You think that after a few visits here you can explain this place? Good luck!" Once a man who was repairing a typewriter for me lost some of his remoteness and said almost angrily that he was astounded at the effrontery of people who felt they could understand a subject or a race or a cult in a few minutes. I told him I felt humble about it, but undaunted, and we talked about how a model can sit in a room with ten painters and have ten different pictures of herself result. "Yes, your picture will not be mine," he said. I said, "I don't want to explain Marseille. I want to try to tell what it does about explaining myself," and we parted amicably, and not for the last time. Now and then taxi drivers have asked me why I stayed in Marseille, and I have told them that I did not want to leave until I had to, and they have either said I was a misguided sentimentalist or have indicated plainly that I should shut up.

The whole implication has been that nobody can understand anything about Marseille except the Massiliotes, as they used to be called. It is almost like the mystique of being a Gypsy. Either you are or you are damned, condemned, blasphemed, as *not*.

This is doubtless true, and in ways too mysterious to probe. But there is no reason why I cannot write about how I, an obvious Anglo-Saxon of American citizenship and birth, must accept the realization that I feel at ease in Marseille. Just as I can shrug off or laugh at the conditioned reactions of many of "us" to the place and its seething movement of people, all held in focus by the phoenix-race bred there since pre-Ségobridgian times, so I can enjoy an occasional soft voice, a reassuring pat on the shoulder. I felt pleased to have a wise old citizen of the town write directly to me in his *Evocations du Vieux Marseille*: "It is like no other town on earth." That is what I need to have him say, because I can never know as well as he does what we both still know.

And it is nice to read, in a letter Mme. de Sévigné wrote to her daughter in 1672,

> I am ecstatic about the peculiar beauty of this town. Yesterday, the weather was heavenly, and the place where I looked over the sea, the fortresses, the mountains, and the city is astonishing . . . I must apologize to Aix, but Marseille is lovelier and livelier than it, in proportion to Paris itself! There are at least a hundred thousand people here; and I cannot even try to count how many of them are beauties: the whole atmosphere makes me somewhat untrustworthy!

Chapter 2

THE CANEBIÈRE

I

The Can o' Beer, as countless English-speaking sailors have long called it, is by now a wide, ugly twentieth-century street that lives in their memories more for what its neighboring alleys offer them than for its own merits. It rises in a gigantic phallic thrust from the Vieux Port eastward toward the hard white hills that much of Marseille is built on, and in spite of its almost bleak lack of beauty, it throbs with vitality drawn from the body of the sea, the ancient riverbed it follows, the people who throng its wide sidewalks and race between its stoplights in every kind of mechanical transportation.

The Canebière has stretched along the path of the ancient sacred stream, the Lacydon, since before A.D. 909, when it was mentioned in a document of the Abbey of St. Victor, or perhaps since 1667 when King Louis XIV ordered new buildings along the path ropemakers had traced to gather hemp from its marshy banks. The whole length, of about a mile,

was until 1928 called by three different names as it rose from
the Old Port to the high hill where Longchamps now spouts
out its beneficent waters, to replace the clogged and dwindling
Lacydon in its ancient fight to cleanse an almost landlocked
little harbor on the salty but nearly tideless Mediterranean.

The Lacydon was revered for its purity, by priests and
people, long before Protis landed near its mouth in about
600 B.C., and even now its name has a watery magic in
Marseille. Little fishing boats and sleek yachts and stylish
clubs and marinas are called for it, and erudite diggers still
probe its fresh-water springs, its banks and prehistoric camp-
sites under concrete and stone and plaster, for artifacts to fix
its dates firmly in history and not fable.

And over the ancient river a flood of traffic now flows, for
many hours of every day. Past midnight a few signs still glare
above the empty sidewalks, but except for the width of them
and the street itself, it looks like any sleepy, small-town
Broadway in Kansas or California.

It comes awake early, with people catching buses or hurrying toward the big railroad station of St. Charles on its
northern hill. By eight it is bustling with shopkeepers heading for business or buyers for the enormous Marché des
Capucins just to the south, or down to the Quai des Belges
to get the pick of the fresh fish. By nine most of the shops
are open: a mixed bag of elegant jewelry stores and cheap
bazaars with tables out on the sidewalk piled with sleazy pants
and cardboard shoes; big chain stores like Monoprix, and a
famous cake shop, and an almost stylish depot catering to
"Ladies of Unusual Build" (i.e., Fat, Skinny); a dozen places
to buy perfumes. There are several small "exchanges," where
for a barely honest fee, money from any nation in the world
can be bought or sold. There are pharmacies, usually with
one old well-dressed lady sitting on a chair as if waiting for

her prescription to be filled, to add respectability to the age-less trade in miracle cures for everything from warts to tertiary syphilis. There are stylish shoe stores and slick travel agencies, busy snack bars, and at the top of the long street, a few movie houses.

Once, about twenty-five years ago, my little girls and I were rambling up the Canebière, pleasantly full of breakfast and already thinking almost subliminally of ordering fresh grilled sardines for lunch, when a nicely dressed young American came from behind us and said, "Excuse me, but I was listening to you folks talk. And I need help."

We were used to a certain amount of panhandling, al-though not in good Chicagoese, and Mary (my direct one) asked, "Are you hungry?"

"Yes," he said. "Yes, I'm really starved. Do you mind if I tell you why?" I readied myself for an old pitch: lost pass-port, got rolled, cable from sick mother.

He walked along beside us, and his story was too good to be anything but true. He had been chosen as Most Promising American Undergraduate by an international "luncheon" club, and for almost two weeks he had been escorted from one French town to another to give a set speech of goodwill ("It mentions Lafayette," he said listlessly) and to sit through endless noonday banquets served in his honor. Every local specialty was produced for his pleasure. In Burgundy, he said, he ate snails four days running and coq au vin, three. In two Alsatian towns he was served *choucroûte garnie* on platters several feet long. Once there was a pig with a glazed apple in its mouth. Somewhere along the line he ate truffles in everything, "even in plain scrambled eggs," he went on as if he were talking to himself.

"I'd be bilious," Mary said, and he said, "No, I really feel

O.K." Then he stopped in his tracks, and said loudly, "But what I want to find out *is*, do you folks know where I can get a hamburger? If I could just eat a hamburger, I'd be all right. Five more days to go . . ."

We went into a huddle on the wide sidewalk, with people skirting us as if we might be contagious or tetched. The children told him that Surcouf made a really fine *boeuf tartare*, if he had enough money, and he said desperately, "That I've got! *Plenty!* But I have to eat a big banquet this noon, and I'll be in some important fellow's house tonight, and all I need is a kind of snack, something to get me through." Then he said, "Would you care to join me, you ladies?"

Anne and Mary loved this overall designation, but grilled sardines lurked somewhere behind the pleasure on their faces. We hated to tell our gastronomical fugitive that we did not know of a single hamburger spot in Marseille, even in Provence; we asked him if he would settle for a fairly good excuse for a hot dog. His face fell and then cheered. We told him how to get to a snack stand near St. Charles. He thanked us with real emotion, and hurried up the Canebière, his head high. The children chided me when I laughed about his problem, and Anne (my hungry one) said she felt quite faint and in fact more so for *food*. . . .

From across the street we read the big signs for porno movies. This was part of the Marseille routine, with my translation of a few words the girls had not yet learned in their convent. Later at lunch we talked again about the boy from Chicago, and decided his trouble might have been worse, if the luncheon clubs had tried to serve him American delicacies like pumpkin pie and fried oysters . . . even hamburgers. . . .

That morning we had stopped for breakfast about a quarter

of the way up the Canebière. We came onto it from our hotel on the first short street to the right, Rue Beauvau, which runs from the big main street three blocks to the Opera. In another short block we passed the monolithic Bourse to the left, and the little Place across from it, bleak and quiet then, with plane trees around it but not showing themselves near the long perspective of the Canebière.

On the west corner of the Place, for a few years into the fifties, one of the last of the street's famous brasseries looked almost like an elegant tearoom, or the solarium of an upper-class English hotel, with comfortable wicker armchairs painted white. It was patronized, however, by firmly French gentlemen of all ages past fifty, respectable but not stodgy. They came in the morning to read their favorite newspapers, before lunch to meet their peers for a mild drink or two, in the afternoon to doze or talk or play cards. There were genteel older ladies at teatime, and attractive younger ones then and perhaps at night, not all of them on the prowl, but apparently meeting people like aunts and lovers. And we went there for breakfast on sunny mornings because it was a fine place to watch the street, and the croissants and café au lait were the best we had yet tasted, indeed the best of our whole lives.

(This paragon of cafés is by now a streamlined publicity office for airplanes, and the only big cafés left on the Canebière are up across from the sad old Hotel de Noailles. They have a dogged air about them: elderly waiters walk tenderly on their hopeless feet; the once grand hotel has a Polynesian cocktail bar, a snack lounge. The few patrons of the café look as if they would rather be in a tiny narrow pinball joint than in spacious dinginess. But across the street under the trees of the Allées de Meilhan, there is the ineffable sight and smell of the Flower Market, three times a week. . . .)

I I

One block up the Can from the Quai des Belges, there is a strange "tourist" shop on the corner of the Rue Beauvau. I knew at first sight that it was not what it seemed, but what it really was I cannot even guess. For years I was aware of the dust on the windowshelves, which thoroughly hid the interior. The little painted clay figures of the Nativity called *santons*, set up in every local household for Christmas and in every gift shop all year 'round for tourists, were uninteresting. The postcards faded irrevocably. The lampshades made of translucent shells lost any dubious allure they might once have had. But there was always a steady come-and-go of thin young men, certainly not dressed for the fishing boats a few dozen feet away.

Once in about 1960 my children wanted to buy a Christmas present for a dear friend who was sitting in a high window at that moment in the Hotel Beauvau, watching the Port. After long study from the sidewalk of the dirty window-shelves, they discovered a tiny silver icebucket with a bottle of champagne packed in cubes of crystal. That was the pre-destined offering, and it was Christmas, and we went in for it.

The man behind the rear counter looked at us with what I charitably adjudged to be amazement, and his few dapper customers slid away. He assured us grudgingly that the wee trinket was costly, but my children had saved some money, and put it out grandly for what was later called at Tiffany's in New York a very valuable *fantaisie*, indeed silver, indeed crystal, and worth fifty times what they had paid. (The adored friend was appreciative but uninterested, although his wife liked it.) Both the shady boss and I were glad when we left, but the little girls were prancing with pleasure, and the trinket, dusty as it was, promised well.

I vowed silently to the puzzled uneasy boss, "I'll never come back to interrupt you," and I never did. But years later when I rounded that corner again, people were dragging a safe and cartons from the little shop, and I felt a pang about the dusty *santons*, the obsolete postcards. I longed suddenly for a little gondola made of polished shells that we had often laughed at: it had a light in it that went on and off, to show a geisha doll lying suggestively in a nest of erect coral spikes. It was marked Hong Kong, of course.

Why had I not bought it? There were two reasons: it was so hellishly quaint as to make me seem affected, especially if I carried it in my limited luggage past the mean-eyed customs inspectors in some place like Los Angeles. And I did not want to go into the strange secret shop again. The man behind the counter had not wanted me to come, and especially not to buy anything. He was pretending to sell tourist stuff, but what was he really selling? Whatever it was, I did not want it. My girls' little silver and crystal toy could have been a password, part of a code? Was he a fence or supplier? What was he really selling?

Certainly we got our money's worth, and judging by the low price we paid, although it seemed like a lot to Anne and Mary, he was glad to get rid of the bit of jewelry and us. The shell gondola, so lewd, still amuses me to regret, but I did not care what new front would occupy that corner on the Canebière, and felt nothing but detachment when, not long ago, I went past the little shop and saw the familiar clutter of trash and possible treasures beyond the dusty windows.

The man was back, I thought without curiosity. And my children were safe, by now.

I I I

Two little blocks up from the Vieux Port, on the right-hand side of the wide street and opposite the gigantic but strange appealing monolith called the Bourse, which can be reached by a blood-curdling pattern of pedestrian crossings, is a pleasant small square currently named for Charles de Gaulle.

The Marseillais, at least the kind I have met during the last couple of decades, plainly do not waste much love on their historical Grey Eminence, and when I would say to a taxi driver, "Place de Gaulle, please," I was unfailingly rebuked with a sardonic correction, "The Place du Gé-né-ra-l de Gaulle, perhaps?" Of course I would agree, sometimes with a weakly muttered, "Sorry," and the rest of the ride would be mutually amicable, or at least not hostile politically.

During the Revolution in the late eighteenth century, there was of course a busy guillotine in the little square, then called Liberté, perforce, but I have never received any cruel vibrations there. Once I lived on a small square in Dijon that had held the public guillotine during the worst years of the Revolution, and the gradual presence of its fear and rage became too strong, and I fled after three months. Nothing ugly ever happened to me on the little Place in Marseille, though, unless one counts human contacts: a Gypsy tapping hopelessly on a taxi window, a terrified tipsy Parisian. People have met there in the sunshine and rain for a long time, for good reasons as well as bad, and by now old women call the benches their own, and knit and watch over their new descendants. Many of them look as if they have sold fish or balloons or hot peanuts along the Quai des Belges in their lustier days, and its sounds still roll up to them, over all the noise of traffic, birds, babies.

The Place de Gaulle has been there since it was laid out in 1784, after the Grand Pavilion of the Arsenal of Galleys was torn down. It was called Place de la Tour, for an important man and not a tower. Later it was Necker, again for politically judicious reasons, and while the guillotine took over, it was logically renamed Liberté, and just as reasonably Impérial during the Empire, and then Royale. After the bulky grandeur of the Bourse rose in the 1860s, it gradually and almost grudgingly became known as the Place de la Bourse by the Marseillais, who liked more glamour in their civic vocabulary. It is interesting to speculate on how they will shake off the present unwelcome name, and for what substitute. . . .

Meanwhile the tidy little square is no longer anything it has ever been before, except that it is everything, with a definitely growing karma about it. It is an easy amble from the Vieux Port, and a short block or two from the Opera and its immediately outlying attractions, ranging from the Cozy-à-Go-Go, with rooms by the hour, day, or week, to the comparatively respectable Hotel Beauvau. Not far away in opposite directions are two of the big covered but open markets that feed the town. There is a glass kiosk like a birdcage on one corner of the Place, bulging with courteous fatherly old cops who help bewildered strangers, of which we are many. There are almost always taxis, with their little cafés across the street from the stand, fumy with *pastis* and with disinfectants from the obligatory toilets.

I have roamed around through the square whenever I was near it, for almost fifty years. I keep an eye on things, like what wars do to little shops. Some are empty now that once looked smart and thriving: a place that sold elegant leather gloves and belts and purses is a snack bar, as I remember . . . something fleeting like that. There used to be an English pub, but War and the Exchange and perhaps the Common Market closed it, as happened to a lot of British pharmacies and bars all along the Côte d'Azur, and now it is bleak and boarded up. Some noble old buildings are "modernized" into one-room studio apartments, and a once-stylish café is now an airline agency.

And one time when the Place was hastily being transformed into a little park for a Christmas present to Marseille, I watched the tall plane trees that ring three sides of it being pruned in what seemed a crazily brutal way. It was painful. They were butchered. Some of us stood outside the barricades and watched with real dismay as the fine trees endured this punishment. Then, magically, for Christmas Eve and the formal opening with its speeches and music, the tall trees turned into *arbres de Noël*, twinkling with thousands of little lights the color of champagne. By now they are still Christmas trees every winter, but lend cool green beauty to everything around them in the summertime, like fashion models, artificially tall and graceful.

After World War II, there seemed to be an extra lot of thin tumblers and jugglers doing shaky handstands on old carpets rolled out on the pavement of what was still the Place de la Bourse, but since about 1971 when the Old Girl got her face lifted again and wore a new if somewhat unwelcome name, she has become a charming if comparatively colorless little square, and it is rather difficult to think of it screaming with furious citizens, running with blood, blazing with firebrands.

Parts of it are a little sunken, but not so much as to be hard on oldsters and toddlers. The modern benches are many, and artfully comfortable. There is water waving musically up from shallow basins. The shrewdly planted shrubbery is low enough to discourage satyrs and agile muggers. (There are few of the latter in a port town dedicated to more serious crime, but no doubt the tidy little park has its fair share of licentious dreamers, even in broad daylight. . . .)

It is a nice place now, very nice, very pretty, and a few years after its latest rebirth it has a pleasant feeling of *being* there, of being accepted . . . at least until another leader can lend his political, emotional, and usually posthumous name to it. It will surely be called less cynically than by its present one. And underneath the new pavements and fountains and perhaps pre-Martian and probably post-hydrogen artifacts called monuments, there will always lie very old bones.

I V

There have been rich invaders in Marseille since the first men found its salty swamps, and it has always made good money for them. That is why its Chamber of Commerce, oldest in France and perhaps the world, is powerful and canny, controlling airports, canals, harbors, tunnels, governed by a constantly renewed body of local merchants with a real doge as their leader, some of them already as subtly Arabian by now as they have been Corsican, Sicilian, Roman, back through the Greeks to the Ségobridgians themselves . . .

After the all-powerful body was formed in 1599, it functioned in several places on the Quai du Port until it moved into the new Town Hall in 1673. It continued to grow, along with the city, and shifted to temporary quarters near where it is now, until Prince Louis Napoleon laid the first stone in 1852 for the present heavy enormous rectangle called La Bourse. In 1860, when he was an emperor at least pro tem, he inaugurated this temple to Man's studiously regulated cupidity, and it still stands, facing what is for a time called the Place de Gaulle.

There is a majestic anchor of great *machismo* in front of the impressive bulk of the temple. Inside, there are hidden delights. On the main floor, in what was meant as a kind of atrium, there is a quite fascinating maritime history of the Old and New Ports, with good maps and models; higher is an excellent public library of the town's past, to be reached and enjoyed at certain times on specified days, and worth every frustrating assault, through long corridors and up endless staircases at the back of the palace; there is even a post office on one side, where I once watched a girl stamp and mail a large flimsy straw hat with a ribbon on it saying "Souvenir de Nice." (This may sound trivial, but her insouciance and the clerk's sardonic acceptance were part of the town.)

Of course ports are places of traffic, in and out, and Marseille has been trafficking in most of our human commodities since before Protis, the Phocean, went there in about 600 B.C.

The Greeks had been stopping along the Mediterranean coast a long time, usually to buy salt before putting out for England and its valuable metals, or perhaps to head directly home again with a full load of the precious stuff. Undoubtedly there was other traffic with the illiterate but canny Ségobridgians: a few coins for a night with a lady, a small amphora of wheat or wine for a night with a girl. Protis was apparently the first sailor to stop in the marshy little harbor and then be paid for *his* favors: the night he anchored his galley, he was offered the King's daughter Gyptis by her own impetuous choice, if he would stay and rule with her. Who could refuse? How could he lose?

This forthright bartering is as intrinsic now as it was then,

in the young captain's powerful new kingdom, and is probably why the first Chamber of Commerce was established in
Marseille almost four hundred years ago. The control has
always been rigidly honorable and cautious, but under its
almost imperial nose a dozen other international markets
have continued to flourish. Not one of them is new. Now
and then, and thanks perhaps to social pressures, some rare
woman can be worth more than olive oil or salt, but at this
moment heroin and cocaine are much more profitable to
handle than "white slaves" ever were. . . .

Marseille is noted, as well as notorious, for its drug traffic.
It is, as it always has been, a perfect center for any such
trading, on the Mediterranean with three ancient continents
at hand, and therefore close to depthless sources of raw material. It has a perfect Old Port, and an impressively efficient
new one, easy of access and therefore of quick exit, with convenient depots in outmoded big villas scattered over the
hills. It is very old, and so it is accustomed and amenable to
every kind of trafficking, neither with open welcome nor
with disapproval and punishment, but with ageless disinter-
est. It is also new and alert, and can offer the most modern
laboratories and processing plants for uncountable amounts
of opium and other raw drugs that are reduced, cut, tricked,
distributed, mostly to the West and perhaps most of all to
the Americas.

Of course some opiates are used in Marseille, as they have
long been on this planet, wherever there is either sated abun-
dance or intolerable misery. (Even the word Canebière is
derived from the Latin one for hemp!) I myself have never
watched any "pushing" there, although I have openly been
offered a fix on Geary Street in San Francisco, and more than
once in women's toilets in luxury hotels from there to New
York and back.

In Marseille, I have never noticed what I would identify as a user or addict in need of his help, although I am sure this cannot be literally so: various forms of human sadness become part of any great scene, and do not stand out. Here at home I have often been depressed or frightened by obvious highs-and-lows of people I have watched or known. But as Joseph Conrad once wrote, the Marseillais are an abstemious race, so that just as he never saw any very fat or very thin townspeople, so have I never been conscious of a badly drugged state in anyone I've seen there. (In this same vein, I have rarely seen a Marseillais more than happily tiddly from wine or *pastis*, although I am sure that alcoholism and drug addiction are commoner than they may have been one or two thousand years ago.)

Of course trade, illicit or straight, breeds its own form of subtle inebriation, and I have watched well-dressed burghers leaving the new Chamber of Commerce, or the great banks near the Place Castellane and the Rond-Point, whose clothes were only a shade more impeccably conservative, whose careful steps were only a shade steadier, than those of their henchmen around the Vieux Port. All of them have the same faces, carefully controlled in public, cold as hawks, with well-massaged jowls and a subtly Caesarean look that means heady power in the old town, as it has since the General himself reduced it to comparative serfdom in a deadly squabble with Pompey in 49 B.C.

These men all possess an intoxicating strength, and are affably courteous when they meet one another at lunch in stylish restaurants. At night it is different, and the so-called leaders of the town, escorting women obviously their wives, never recognize their shadier counterparts, as obviously dining with beautiful Scandinavian ski bunnies down from Davos or costly-looking Paris mannequins "resting" in Nice. The traders' faces are different with sundown: more socially cautious on the one hand, on the other more arrogantly relaxed. The next morning, though, masks fit on again, and barter in international oil stocks as well as heroin, race horses, and girls will go on addictively, as it has for almost too long to recall.

According to local and even worldwide reports, traditional mob control has lost its power in Marseille crime levels. There are apparently no solid leaders; worse yet, a single one is missing, the *capo*, the *chef*. Instead, many small groups, their goons inept spratlings in an ancient shark-infested sea, fumble through petty holdups and car thefts and riots, mostly in neighboring provincial towns, or simply "wait around," as the Pinball Boys seemed doomed to do, pandering a little, betting punily, snoozing off the caffein shakes.

Meanwhile, the vulpine traders and their henchmen keep an eye on the general state of things, perhaps waiting like many other earthlings for another Capone or Hitler. Business is good, although in flux: cocaine, hash, and heroin sell well in the West, but sexual permissiveness has hurt the flesh market.

Local Catholics are bitter against Protestants about their apparent tolerance of this new promiscuity. Protestants are equally bitter about Romish "charity" toward the insane acceptance of "Arab" citizens since the Algerian troubles in the early 1960s. Both religious groups in turn are openly hostile and even vicious about denouncing the Communists for all this. Trade suffers, but continues.

And the honored Marseillais who carry on their long supervision of the many-colored commerce of the city know almost atavistically that ideological strife has never much hurt the market. They have been appointed to four-year terms in the Chamber to "guard and defend their fellow-citizens on land and sea," and since 1599 have done so. If they must share their fashionable tailors with the traders they smile to at lunch at the Jambon de Parme or the Pescadou and then cut dead at dinner in the New York, they act with one eye on their city's honor and the other on its prosperity. Their mystical fortress, the Bourse, is behind them.

The palatial Bourse itself has had its whole face washed, slowly, side after side. It has been scrubbed and scraped, a gigantic and tedious cosmetic process all round, and especially on the Canebière façade, with its heroic statues stonily enduring most intimate explorations for soot, bird lice, mildew, and related grime. For a few decades now it may look somewhat friendlier and less austere than when it sulks behind city dirt, but never more ponderously important. The little square across the street remains subject to frequent changes of names, depending upon the times, but it seems inconceivable that the enormous fortress of the old-young Bourse will not signify commercial security for several centuries more, to the canny citizens who trust in it as a potent symbol.

V

A little farther up the Canebière from the Bourse is the Cours St. Louis, a pretty leafy Place that in good weather teams with snack stands and with people eating at them, eating on the *café-terrasses,* eating on the curbs. It all smells good and stays tidy, because who buys food and then throws it away? And across the Canebière is the Cours Belsunce, with the noble Port d'Aix at its far north and a big fish stand down at the hectic entrance. Traffic lights there turn red and green, cars stop or screech ahead in the inimitably hellish music of any such intersection in France, and people go right on choosing their squid or scallops from the cool seaweedy piles of them on the corner. In summer, when the stand is closed, it seems strange to turn into the Cours Belsunce without its whiff of clean subtle brininess.

All the crossings along the Canebière are hair-raising to a stranger, because of the astonishing speed the cars can attain in a few feet from a dead stop, and although there are zones marked for pedestrians in several places, it is recommended (by me as well as any other visitor claiming average intelligence and survival wishes) to spot the traffic lights and use them. There are three or four, and they are worth the extra footage to reach them. And once across the wide Canebière and safely onto the sidewalk again, one feels mystically *younger.* . . .

A good place to cross, except perhaps during the meal hours, is up in front of the vaguely drab old Noailles café, where the Boulevards Dugommier and Garibaldi meet at the Canebière. The Noailles is a fine place to sit, after a late morning survey of the Flower Market, which is always crowded, even in any rain but a downpour. People look dazed by its fresh beauty. They buy whatever flowers are in season, and every kind of nursery planting in the spring, every kind of dry root bush or tree in the fall. They buy things in pots. They take their own containers and supervise the skillful gardeners who fill them. They gather around a collection of succulents, and then drift on to look speculatively at some rare hideous begonias.

On about June 24, there used to be a Garlic Fair along the enchanted Allées, and dealers came from all over France to choose their year's supply of the virile herb. Famous restaurateurs were there, and unknown housewives, and if the wind was right, the wonderful light whiff of all the ivory ropes of the stuff could be caught as soon as one turned up from the Quai des Belges. By now the Fair has been moved a little south of the Canebière, but it can still be smelled out, and it still is exciting.

And from the first Sunday in December, there is the Foire des Santons. It is unique, which means normal in Marseille. Dozens of booths are lined up under the bare trees of Les Allées. There are beautiful *santons* from human size to one-half inch, by local *santonniers* as well as any other reputable artists in the country or in the world, and there are many clumsy, undistinguished kinds alongside, painted garishly or left plainly in the baked "red earth of Provence stained with the Saracens' blood."

Weekends are liveliest as Christmas approaches, of course, with families choosing additions to their own crêches or buying new characters of the Nativity story for their friends, but perhaps the best (or strangest) time to go along Les Allées is after the holidays. Many of the stands have closed and moved away for another year. A few old women in layers of wool and thick felt boots stand hopefully behind their little counters. At first they seem to have almost nothing to sell. Then they begin to pull out broken shoeboxes and grimy paper sacks filled with flawed tiny images. Some of them are pitiful, or plainly prankish. Once I bought a two-inch *santon* of a famous character in the Nativity play, the village simpleton. When he looks up at the Star blazing in the sky, his jaw drops, his eyes roll, and he raises his hands mutely toward Heaven. This time, though, a mischievous *santonnier* had neatly turned his arms downward, at the elbows, so that his ecstatic upward gaze and his earthy gesture were shockingly at odds. At first I thought this heathenish little joke was funny. But before I took the *santon* home, I let it fall onto a tile floor and be shattered.

There were other small tricks that had been pulled, perhaps by naughty apprentices, and gradually the old women brought them out, looking casual but with a sharp eye on my reactions. Most of the dolls were unpainted. There were wee dogs with five legs, and some shepherds with only one. A sow a few inches long lay on a pancake of clay suckling ten piglets that were really kittens. I bought a rooster with his head on backward. With a little patience it would be easy to assemble a small-scale Nativity worthy of Hieronymus Bośch, or perhaps Salvador Dali . . . and it was interesting that the crowds of jolly, pushing Christmas shoppers had intuitively rejected all these mistakes. I took several back to California to give to people, but by the time I got home, their first strange humor had vanished, and they seemed almost evil.

And, as always, the windows of the dim old Café de Noailles are the best place to watch the Foire . . . warm and lively in the winter holidays, even at night. People come in with their children, and compare their *santons* over orange sodas and *pastis*, according to their ages. Thin "Arabs" drink tea silently. The elderly waiters move slightly faster, and the fat cashier is almost pretty in her best clothes. Down the winding stairs, the mysterious subterranean toilets rumble and shudder as usual, under the traffic of the big intersection.

The Noailles is most familiar to me at noon, though, in winter or any other season. Then the people run wildly homeward for their two-hour meals, and on Flower Market days they carry big bunches of tulips, say, or a flat of pansies. Once I saw a very short Oriental girl totter toward the café and then across the Canebière onto the Boulevard Garibaldi, under an enormous pot with a rubber plant in it, taller than she was. I watched her with amazement and alarm, but under her black silk trousers her knees were not even buckling.

This corner café is a prime place to look for a peculiar

color of hair dye that was popular in 1973 but almost rare three years later. I call it Canebière Red, and like to assume that it is the same "henna" that was used two thousand and more years ago. It is almost purple in its shadows, and is more orange than scarlet. It seems to make female hair stiff and coarse, like the stuffing in a very old mattress. Many middle-aged women used it in '73, even elderly fishwives from the Quai des Belges. Mostly it was seen, though, on tough girls of twenty or so, the kind that made no bones about being what they were . . . mixed blood, African, Gypsy, Indo-Chinese, candles burning bright and fast. By now this unique color has grown out, faded, perhaps even been shaved off to help cheap wigs fit better. The few women one spots from the old Noailles who still wear it are otherwise like others of their general class, short heavy sensible people, who would have their hair dyed black again if they had not invested too much in 1973 for Canebière Red.

And past Les Allées and their elegant old bandstand, now a publicity office run by the city, the Canebière seems to end logically with a huge church, set obliquely on the rising ground, called St. Vincent de Paul or "Les Réformés" or its more correct name of Les Augustins-Réformés. It is typically Marseillais, in its tongue-in-cheek bravura, for although it looks pure Northern Gothic of about the thirteenth century, it was built just in time to be dedicated in 1867. It still remains impressive: plainly an ecclesiastical joke, but not a shoddy one . . . perhaps a trick, but not a lie! Like the *santons* of the wintry fair below it in the Allées, it is noble as well as subtly prankish, a fitting comment on the street it dominates.

Chapter 3

PORT AND QUAYS

I

The Old Port of Marseille has always been an ideal small harbor, which of course used to seem much bigger than it does now. It is a neat oblong, going in from the Mediterranean Sea to what was once the mouth of the Lacydon and is now the Quai des Belges, with the Quai du Port on its left, and the Rive Neuve to the right.

When Protis landed somewhere along the swampy shores in about 600 B.C., the settlement of fishermen and saltmakers was relatively simple. By now, of course, the city is commonly dubbed tough and evil, which I doubt that he found it.

Marseille is tough, all right, the way all big ports must be. The people who have stayed there for so long are uncompromising in the way they face the sea for their livelihood. And Marseille is evil, the way all big ports have always been, for lonely sailors must put in there for a few hours or a night or two, and they need women and other kinds of warmth, and

know or are quickly told where to get it. But the toughness
and the evil, so-called, have never scared me, because they
are intrinsic to the strength and dignity I have always felt
there. This respect is difficult to transfer to anyone, and sometimes impossible.

People say, "Oh, don't go to Marseille. Don't bother."
People from as close to this mysterious city as Aix-en-Provence
say, "Don't go there! It is a dreadful place." People, mostly
from England or New York, say, "*Marseille! Nobody* goes
there!" (The English say Marsales.)

But I do go there. I have been returning almost helplessly
to the Old Port since my first stay there in 1929, and have
always felt the same inner acceptance and exhilaration. When
I lived in Aix for a few years with my two young girls, we
went on the bus to Marseille as eagerly as if it were a kind
of escape hatch from the requisite gentility of the old Royalist
town, and its convents and bells and fountains and schools.
And when I finally stayed near the Port for several months instead of a few days or weeks, and could ask people to meet
me there, I was astounded by their responses to the invitation
itself, and then to what they found if they dared come that
far (everything from a few kilometers to several thousand,
not counting the hovercraft over the Channel and dock
strikes in New York and suchlike modern gimmicks).

In general what they felt was good-to-fine, with mutual
easiness and communion. In one case, though, a long friend-
ship may well have drifted brutally onto the rocks. Marseille was too powerful for the tenuously strong relationship
that had been kept alive through rare exchanges of letters
and parcels and even visits through World War II and before
and after. Ropes snapped almost visibly while our Scottish
friends were in the town, and they cut themselves free in
near-panic, a few days ahead of the scheduled end of their

visit, and headed toward Paris like rescued sailors, breathing hard and glancing behind them now and then.

My sister and I were living in a two-room flat, the kind with a gas-plate for cooking in the bathroom and a superb view over most of the Vieux Port, so we got a room for our friends at the Beauvau on the Quai des Belges at the land end of the Port. They could see the whole thing a few floors below them: the constant movement of the fishing boats, the morning market of everything that swims or creeps or sits underwater along the Mediterranean shores, the people, the two sides of the Port: that is, the most exciting view in the world, or one of them.

They were plainly not quite comfortable. We thought it was because they were tired. Then we thought it was because they really mistrusted French food and were not used to drinking much wine and were constitutionally (historically) averse to "the French" as such. Soon, though, it was plain that they were actually timid about being in Marseille, center of the White Trade to South America, Arab terrorists, smuggling, and now heroin. They had heard of what was going on, they finally told us, and it seemed fairly clear that they had come to persuade us to leave this place, if not for our own sakes for those of our departed parents, whom they had both known.

My sister and I are chronologically mature people, I at least to the point of overripeness, but I know that these two dear friends were persuading us, urging us, to leave, to escape with them in their comfortable car, to get out of this peculiarly wicked place while we could. It was as if we were two runaway teenagers, and we both felt some of their loyal concern for our safety, but went blandly walking home at night from the Opera or filthy movies like *The Last Tango in Paris* (along well-lighted streets and purposefully of course, and together!), and sitting in cafés drinking degenerate apéritifs before lunch, and prowling around the piles of rescued stones at the government reconstructions going on at the Abbey of St. Victor and Paul Puget's great building of the municipal poorhouse, La Vieille Charité. How could these two nice young girls have become so careless and so blind? they wondered in balloons over their uneasy heads.

They told us that several friends had said jokingly before they left England, when they admitted they were going to Marseille, "How mad! *Nobody* goes to Marseille! But be sure to bring us back a pocketful of Big H, if the bullets miss you! . . . some top-quality fixes, old boy!" And they told us more than once how when one returns to England, if there is any mention of having been in or near Marseille, one is held in Customs, for drastic investigation.

We tried to be gentle and thoughtful about it, and planned little picnics and nice meals at places they would like, preferably with no view at all except at a safe minor mural from Italy to reassure them. The lusty little fish places along the Rive Neuve were very upsetting to them, in a completely discreet way, and we knew that both of them had been suffering at the Beauvau from expected and awaited gastric distress after our two or three such sorties. . . . We decided that the main trouble on the quays was that people walked along the sidewalks and looked in to see what everybody was eating and then read the menu and then either came in or walked farther along, while a trained female barker at the door cajoled and insulted them. We were used to this, after so many years and months, but it was too embarrassing to the visitors, and we settled for upper-level somewhat elegant restaurants with muted lights and soft views of Venice in the sunlight or the moonlight or at dawn, and *no windows.* . . .

One day, though, my sister and I proposed to show them

the ruins of the Vieille Charité, which are gradually being put together again according to Puget's golden dream. It will take another twelve years, perhaps, and when it is done, with the strange chapel in the middle of the galleried court, it will be a school for students of the communications media . . . film, television, radio, printing, everything. It is another fine plan, and we knew our friends were aware and educated about ecclesiastical architecture, and we wanted them to see the gradually revivifying core, the chapel. It was a reassurance of the human spirit, to Norah and me, and perhaps it would be to them too.

It was a bright day, and we walked up to the Place des Moulins at the top of the hill, past things like the Maison Diamantée and of course the exquisite Town Hall, and the Scots were lively and interested. Naturally we had to climb through quite a lot of sordid crooked streets, in the quarter that is now mostly Arab because it is old and ill-furnished with what human beings are supposed to require for modern life. But up at the top, on the austere little square, there was the sound of children playing in the grammar school, and we looked pleasurably at the remnants of the two or three remaining stone mills and then headed down toward the old poorhouse.

It is a big hollow block, with small windows now toothy with broken glass on the outside walls, and a medieval-looking tipped grating over the sidewalks to keep stones from falling on the passersby, that hangs out, strangely hostile and evil. One can't help looking up at it, and my sister, who hates rats dead or alive, was sickened to see three withered bodies of them lying on the coarse wires. They could have been there for a week or ten years, and could have been tossed out by tenants or simply been suicidal.

There is only one entrance to the Charité, I think . . . that is, the kind a carriage could go through, to bring a doctor or a municipal officer. And immediately one sees the chapel in the center of the enormous courtyard, and the lacework of all the galleries running around it. The usual mournful guard was not there, and we poked around the piles of numbered and labeled stones that had been pulled down by Beaux Arts students working on the reconstruction, and I think that our friends were for a time happy and easy in their skins. She toyed with the possibility of taking perhaps one tiny stone home with her, an idea we all discouraged firmly, and then we encouraged him when he said he planned to read about Paul Puget, once home again. We left unwillingly.

We walked down the crooked steep streets, sometimes only staircases, and there were wispy good smells of hot couscous and fish in the air. We turned toward the sea, and came out below the Cathedral and then went to a café called something funny like Le San Francisco and drank an *apéro* in a mild gale: orange squash for them, and my sister and I ordered dry vermouth.

We were very hungry, and with prearrangement we headed our tired friends toward a place under the arcades along the Quai du Port, where the old quarter used to be that was detonated during the war. The blocks of new buildings are hideous, but arcades are always good, and it was satisfying to be in the shade after our windy drink out at the end of the Port. My sister walked ahead with the lady, and I loitered a little with her husband, because I had known him a long time and wanted to reestablish a connection that had suddenly, after all the years of student exchanges, war, bombings, stress, fellowships, all that, perhaps been cut off by an accident in place rather than in time.

He leaned toward me confidentially, although the two others were at least a hundred yards ahead of us, and said,

"You know, my dear, I . . . we . . . really don't mind too dreadfully the dirty gutters in these old slums, and the piles of fruit skins in corners and the washing hung out of the windows. We know that the underprivileged are always somewhere." He chuckled a little. "I must say your poor sister was a bit startled by those dead rats hanging over our heads though!"

"She has a slight phobia about them in general, dead or live," I said.

"Of course, of course," he went on firmly. "But I do think these people down here where things are nicer should wash the blood off the pavements."

It was plain to me that I was already somewhat defensive, and for a flash I dismissed this criticism as part of the whole fiasco and decided not to look down. Then I remembered what a brave man our friend had always been, and what he saw during all the bombings in England when he was one of the chief fire wardens, and I knew at once that the dry brown splatters under my feet were indeed old blood, and then that they came from one of the dozens of narrow cafés under the arcades, and I made myself say casually, "Oh, yes . . . there was a bad shooting there a few days ago, but you'd think they'd swab down the sidewalk before now. Perhaps it's for publicity. Ghoulish . . ."

I knew that I was putting my foot in my mouth . . . one more proof that my sister and I had lost all our good middleclass standards of behavior, to be able to stroll past a gory den without a visible shudder!

"I suppose it was connected with the drug traffic," our friend said, trying in a subtly disapproving way to match my nonchalance, and a little triumphant that at last he had proof of what everybody at home had warned him about. He took my arm after we got past the stains, and murmured, "Let's not say anything about this to the others. . . ."

We did not, but he was right, and as if meant by the gods I had taken him straight to the proof of everything he knew in his bones about Marseille.

We had passed the Tanagra, one of the countless deep bars that have emerged as naturally as mushrooms from dung, along the Quai du Port, under the new/old arcades. About four days before we went by, two men had come in and gunned down, in what was generally referred to in the press as "American-style," the barmaid-owner named something like Rita, a goodlooking and apparently innocent young man drinking his first or tenth espresso, and two known informers or henchmen in one of the many small gangs that seem to have supplanted any firm organization of crime in Marseille. The gunsels then left, calmly. I forget whether they were later arrested. Nobody seemed to be much annoyed by any- thing except the fact that the act was one of petty revenge carried out by amateurs. Where was the old spit and polish in crime? lamented the editorials in everything from *Le Meridional* to *L'Express*. Marseille might be the great center for the American drug market, but it was sadly lacking in local solidarity, and panache.

Well, what with *la patronne* shot dead beside her coffee machine, and all the fuss about fingerprints and so on, the sidewalk never got washed, and the little sad café was closed and dark as we hurried past it toward the ladies, my sister and our friend. It seemed odd that I had not thought much about the Tanagra. I knew about the almost nonchalant gun- ning, and I understood why it was called "American-style," with chauvinistic regret that it could not have been labeled Sicilian or Sardinian or Algerian, or . . . And the little bar and its hapless owner and customer were just across the Old Port from where we lived. But we had never thought about going there or *not* going there to see about the blood, and suddenly we had done so!

All this was too complicated to explain to my plainly troubled friend. He said hastily before we went into the restaurant and joined the two women, "You know, my dear, we do worry dreadfully about you, here in all this," and I said urgently, "Please don't worry!" and we sat down . to what turned out to be the best meal of their stay there. He and I had a secret, valiantly kept, and his wife and my sister were as blandly ignorant as well-fed geese about it. But all the time I was thinking of the Pinball Boys, and petty crime that can turn vile, and the mystery of what I clumsily call the karma of a place.

I I

Now, when you read about the Occupation, or the blastings done with municipal consent by the Invaders in 1944, or the takeover of the American-style gangsters since then, with perhaps a municipal wink, it is all revolvers, submachine guns, hands-up-face-to-wall, who ratted on whom, and an unborn resistance of some 2,500 years, at least in certain parts of Marseille like the section back of the Quai du Port.

One Sunday in 1973, down on the wide and active Quai, and in toward the city from the Tanagra where my shaken Scottish friend and I had stepped firmly over the dried blood in front of the narrow little bar, there were the usual crowds of a bright spring holiday . . . clots of people watching a man trying to sell watches, a woman twisting peanuts into an odorous bowl of boiling caramel for people watching her and already munching. There were wild posies of balloons, and stands selling dreadful nougat and fried Algerian sweets. Certainly there would be a shell game going on, set up with a couple of big empty paper cartons and involving three little paper cups or empty tomato-paste cans, and a thick crowd of men watching some fellow gull being robbed. It seemed part of an almost innocent *voyeurisme*: "He is dumber than I am! I would have known where the peanut, or the two-franc piece, or the old dice was. I would have known all the time. . . ."

My sister Norah and I liked to dawdle and watch, as did anyone who went to the long buzzy Quai on a Sunday. We stopped now and then. There was one young man with a rather exhausted-looking woman, a dramatically thick bandage over her eyes, who would intone magic numbers when they were "thought" by the quiet but cynical audience. (Drifters like us are tough, except for our basic gullibility and friendliness!)

Norah expressed real or at least conditioned pleasure at seeing this kind of cheating encouraged and permitted so openly; it was one of the few lasting pleasures, one of the rare liberties left to us, she said firmly.

Farther along the Quai, about across from the rosy perfection of the old Town Hall, there was the usual crowd of silent watchers in their Sunday clothes, around the usual man manipulating his usual shell game on top of his pile of paper cartons. We went toward his back, where there was a thinned ring of people, so that we could hear him con, or try to con, all of us.

Surprisingly, he seemed to have a helper, a burly but slick-looking man in a light coat. The two stood close together, murmuring to each other and to a third fellow facing us, with his sharply cut suit turned backside to the noncommittal watchers. I thought in an almost hilarious way that never had I seen such perfect casting and lighting for a low-grade gangster movie. The back of the shell-game man, and then the two profiles muttering to him, were heavy, clean, dangerous, with an acute wariness about them. One man wore the sensitive but thick carving of a Roman, a pip-squeak Mussolini, with arching lips and cold veiled eyes.

Down the Quai, past the toylike Town Hall, was the one-of-a-hundred tiny bars where the four people had died lately, and still I continued to feel amused and silly about how trite the casting was for any and all such underworld melodrama, so wasted here on the Quai for a meaningless shell game. My sister continued to explain the beauties of such legal freedom, where men could drink or not, get bellyaches on sugared peanuts if they wished, bet on which nutshell has a pea under it, all along the lapping waters of the Old Port, the bounds of the ageless Lacydon. Moral freedom, she said.

The two new men leaned close to the shell man, whispering, their eyes darting every way over the silent ring of watchers. For a second I thought with a strange dismay that they were smarter than the average lot of the gulls, and as such were challenging him about some money he had not repaid them on their one lucky guess. (They were two-to-one, and bigger—)

Suddenly the quiet crowd stepped back, right in front of us, and the three men went past us so fast that I did not really see them, until they were across the wide street and into the paddy wagon, the shell man pushed politely into the back and the two plainclothesmen with their cold Italianate faces pinched into the front part.

As they slipped past us in the crowd, a small thin rat of a man whispered to me with an emanation of glee, and with his long wrists crossed suddenly in front of him, "The cops! He's manacled!" This seemed to delight him. And sure enough, the quiet crook or victim or whatever he was, the nondescript man we had often seen moving three small tin cans or paper cups around on top of his old cartons, had his short arms helplessly locked behind him, so that he had to be boosted up into the police wagon before the door was slammed on him.

The silent crowd seemed to have a gigantic word written above it in another comic-strip balloon. It looked vacantly, impersonally, at the old cartons. Then it straggled this way and that along the Quai, and the top box blew off toward the water. My sister and I went along toward the sea, not talking about human freedom or anything else. We felt as mute, inwardly, as everyone else had seemed to be.

Later, on the last ferry across the Vieux Port to our side, we talked with a certain awe of the perfect casting of the two plainclothesmen . . . except for their eyes, we said, those cold eyes suddenly unveiled, no longer looking stupid enough to play the shell game, trained to watch for the trick that inevitably would be tried, open in the crowd of watching sheep. Until those two chosen men had lifted their reptilian lids, narrow and quick, they looked like the rest of the Marseillais on Sundays on the Quai du Port: sharp clothes, the kind that will do for weddings and then for funerals with a different tie, a close holiday shave and some pomade on the hair, too much noon dinner. But once they moved in, they showed their snake-eyes, and did not hide them again, even though their backs were calmly turned on the thick crowd around the two cartons, the three cups, the lonely gambler.

In some other place (what more likely one than there?), at some time (although when as well as then, with crowds around on a brisk day of celebration?), we might have had a rattle of bullets, bigger than the one at the little Tanagra where only four people died with a lot of blood, or there might have been knives drawn and women scuttling for shelter with their babies, as happens everywhere every day. But this was all very calm, and the back of the middle-aged shell man looked silent and resigned, as he sped almost expertly between the two detectives toward the safe wagon.

Probably he served in the great game of Liberty and Free-dom, as my sister saw it, as a kind of catalyst. As I myself prefer to use it in my own self-dramatization, he was front man, helpless, a patsy for passing signals and so on to at least one organized band along the Quai du Port. His crowds, many of them well paid to stand there stolidly and draw other goons, made easy go-betweens for messages and signals and small packets of drugs. Perhaps he even made a little honest shell money on the side, from his own game, that is.

There was a general feeling that he was hardly more permanent a character there than we were—at least on that quay so much older than all of us.

I I I

Some of the many small bars along the Quai du Port have been there ever since the monotonously matching apartment houses were built after that area was blown up to cleanse the planet of one of its most thriving and pestilential sores. (Success, if any, was temporary.)

The new buildings, designed heavily but to the same height as the exquisite old City Hall in their center, and with arcades running along the street level and with decent-sized balconies, seem to be occupied by every type of tenant, judg-ing by the furnishings of the port side of the apartments.

Some of them are discreet exercises in static symmetry, at least seen from fifty feet below, with four potted dwarf cypress, two imitation Roman tubs filled with whatever beauties the florist can supply and the beating summer sun and occasional cruel mistral will let survive, and even an occasional head of a faun or fragment of a neo-Pompeian mosaic, depending on the purse and proclivities of the flats' occupants, who could be local retired soap manufacturers or Parisian decorators. And some of the balconies are hung continually with bright laundry, as in the enormous *"cités"* on the outskirts of Marseille and every other big town of France, and that means that the people who live there are fairly poor as well as clean. On the Vieux Port it also means, most often, that they are Algerians, some Arabs as they are called with varying shades of meaning, and some repatriated *pieds noirs*, or Viet refugees.

These newcomers, when they can house themselves decently in such apartments as line the Quai du Port, are fastidiously clean, and they are usually very poor indeed. And many of their sons go downstairs to the tiny crowded bars, as they would probably be doing in North Africa or Saigon if they could still be there. . . .

The bars look as alike as houses in a low-income American suburb, so that one wonders how their occupants or habitués know Bide-a-Wee from Dunrovin in East Colusa, Idaho, or La Lune Bleue from Bébé-à-Go-Go under the arcades along the Quai. They are a new phenomenon, much smaller than those prewar pubs that always had steamy windows and the quiet clickings from a billiard table toward the back, and men playing long slow card games on tables with thick cloth covers. These new espresso joints are almost pinched in size, and stuffy with cigarette smoke, and very noisy.

They smell alike, of bitter coffee from the innumerable tiny cups that are their standard drink, of strong tobacco, occasionally of disinfectant from the toilet at the back end. And they sound alike, because of the jukebox music that seems to pick itself up from one café to the next, in a broken blaring rhythm that is not unpleasant if one can move along outside, and not be in with the immediate beat and the urgent stench and the look of chromium and rigid nearness that is dictated by the space the cafés are crowded into. They all have a long very narrow bar, running from the sidewalk to the back, where there is a legally required sign saying Telephone-Toilets, although trying to use either of them is inadvisable. There are usually two or three minuscule tables along the other side of the room; again a legal order? There must always be a cigarette vendor. And there are two or even several wildly lighted pinball machines.

There are of course countless native-born men in an old port the size of Marseille, with a current population of about one million, and they are of every size and shape and color. There is, however, a strongly *typical* size-shape-color of some Marseillais, and it is easy and strangely heartening to recognize one immediately. He is short, broadly built, with very strong arms and legs on a long torso, and he has black eyes and hair and often a nutlike shade of skin. His voice is deep. He emanates a feeling of male power, quiet but unquestioning. When he is not working at the intense and almost unceasing job of being a fisherman or perhaps a mason, he is with a woman built almost exactly like him, and although their children are skinny in their first years, they soon grow into the same adult mold as their parents and their forebears for more than two thousand years.

That is why it is puzzling about the Pinball Boys, the slender hollow-chested dandies who seem to spend twenty hours a day in the small smoky cafés under the arcades, and perhaps in other quarters of Marseille. Where did they come from? They are often tall, with white fingers, and silky hair worn to their narrow shoulders. It seems improbable that they are the sons of the tough blunt men and women who are intrinsically Marseillais, and it is true that in smaller towns in Provence, and perhaps everywhere in France, their pale twins lean against the same bars and drink the same endless tiny cups of espresso, and pull languidly at the pinball buttons. They are too young to be a ghastly result of wartime spawnings. They are too frail to have been bred by working people or real peasants, and most of all, they are too much *alike*, in their long bones and cavernous and sometimes pretty faces, to be a local phenomenon, something unique to one part of this or any other town.

As French youths, they are supposed to have been subjected to some kind of vocational training after their enforced years of primary education, so that they can say they know the rudiments of truck driving or baking or hairdressing. On the streets near the technical schools in Marseille, for instance, it is easy to recognize young people who are preparing for this or that kind of trade: they are busy or preoccupied or worried, and they are in a hurry, and they look as if they will turn into solidly built sane adults, no matter how slow they may be mentally. The Pinball Boys, though, are another breed, and besides wondering where they came from, from what and whence they sprang, one ponders on how they manage to survive now, putting endless coins into all the machines, and what will possibly and probably become of them. Certainly they look eminently susceptible to the dangers of fresh air . . . or of steady employment.

Fortunately the customers who can fit into the tiny cafés are as thin as skeletons, and young and restless enough to prefer standing or leaning to sitting. They move with accomplished deftness from bar to jukebox and back, leaving their little cups here and there. If they have their girls with them, they share an occasional cigarette as a grudging sign of possession, I suppose, and since there are no ashtrays, the floors become almost stylishly filthy by midafternoon of a swinging Sunday. The girls never seem to stand up by "les pinballs," as they are called in Franglais, or show any interest in them or the players: it is probably something about the unwritten laws of local *machismo?* They sit at the puny tables, or in good weather out on the sidewalk terraces, with one or two other chicks dressed exactly like them, whose men are inside gaming. The girls usually drink cokes or bottled fruit pop; they always pay for this debauchery, but never for their cigarettes . . . *machismo* again.

Their boyfriends dress alike, too, in light-colored suits with pinched waists. In the seventies their shirts are dark and their ties exaggeratedly wide and soft, boldly striped. Their hair is more long than short, with elaborate sideburns, and few of them wear either beards or handlebars, probably because the times and they are not yet ripe enough. They have narrow closed faces, and it seems the style for them to keep their eyes narrowed too, as if light, or perhaps reality, should be as shut out as possible. There is a general roar of talk, especially around the jukeboxes, but it is not deep and robust, as in the neighborhood pubs their elders go to.

Outsiders, people like innocent tourists or even locals desperately needing to make a telephone or natural call, can come in and through without a break in the mechanical support of the machines and the hissing of the monstrous coffee-makers, whereas in an old-fashioned bar almost any stranger will cause a moment or so of dead silence, before the natural decibels pick up again. The young men along the Quai du Port seem deliberately unaware of intrusion, at least momentarily, as if they were practicing to be cool 1930s gangsters, and they never laugh, or move their faces much when they talk. When they spit out or drop their cigarette butts, they never step on them, as if that were a kind of code or password, a *proof* of something.

It is foolish to bother to check such an unimportant fact as the number of espresso bars along the Quai in 1973 or 1976, as compared with 1970 when I was first aware of them, but there do seem to be at least twice as many, and this may be either the cause or the result of the current need for loud mechanized games in restless puzzled young men. It is noticeable in small towns in Provence, where thin boys drift into the small bars as soon as the older men go off to work after their morning coffee or nip, and stay there in seeming aimlessness until the places close at night. And of course if one holds to the theory that every great city is made up of a thousand villages, the arcades along the Vieux Port are surely as much a small community as Luynes or Sâlon or Les Arcs. The only real difference is that in Marseille the espresso joints seem to belong solely to the young. There is no risk of their ever smelling of the *pastis* that older men rely on for their refreshment and, some claim, their virility. There seems even less risk that the narrow-faced, narrow-hipped boys around the pinballs will someday work in the fishing fleet that beats like a gigantic heart across the sidewalk from the bars, on the ever-changing waters of the Vieux Port.

At best, they might become occasional salesmen of supercharged pleasure boats or secondhand sports cars, or perhaps qualify gradually as members of any number of fringe "clubs" of the big dope business there. But they are simply not built to work as the older men do: they are lighter and longer, and more prone to broken bones and chest pains. They seem to have enough money for one sharp suit, several espressos a day, slugs for the machines, and an occasional date. They look geared to a drop-out defeatism.

It is presumptuous to surmise, and such an opinion as this one is based rashly and solely on casual observation over a few years in small towns in Provence. Of course there have always been drifting do-less unemployed youths, uninterested in working at a trade or in more education than the law has forced them to accept. But lately, at least along the Quai du Port, the number seems greater, and therefore the demand for more places for them to huddle in has been satisfied with countless small noisy smoky bars. And the lodestone, the odor of civet and musk, the siren's song, seems to be the impersonal clashing tickle of the pinballs, a rhythm that sounds above the juke music and the steam from the espresso machine, and that reduces the human voice to a thin futile yell. It makes a security blanket, a womb.

Chapter 4

SOME OF THE
WOMEN

I

Of course there are many kinds of women in Marseille, as everywhere, and they can fairly easily be bracketed according to their physical structures, their ways of living, their jobs, their accents. This soon becomes true in any settlement of people, whether it be a one-year-old subdivision "market-plaza" in Southern California, with its own post office and pharmacy and laundromat, or the quarters around the Vieux Port in a city twenty-six hundred times older.

I have never known the remaining aristocrats in Marseille, although I have read some of their books and probably seen them in a few restaurants and theatres. Their class never stays long in such a tough town: several kings and princes have been scared frantic by it, and the gaudy shows put on for their weddings and crownings and suchlike festivals were more cake than bread for the people's turbulent and often truculent hungers. The peers of the land are mostly transitory.

The upper class now seems based on how much soap was sold a hundred years ago, the famous oily *savon de Marseille,* and on how that much soap has made money enough to buy shares in gasoline companies around Martiques and the Etang de Berre, and now around Fos, the new industrial city promised by international tradesmen-in-commodities to relieve some of the pressure of the old and new ports of the ancient city, both in traffic and in population, as well as in hard cash.

The middle classes, if one can follow the old line of including people like lawyers, merchants, town officials, doctors, bankers (perhaps they should go up a notch financially?), live and eat well in Marseille, and are usually native-born and more or less devoted to the place . . . or at least more active about their public love for it. I saw many of them, over the past decades, on the streets and in the stylish and even low-class brasseries and cafés, and especially in the good restaurants, where they ate a lot at midday and turned pink, even under forty. The pinkest were the youngest, it seemed to me: they were trying hard to keep up with the hard-eyed city politicos they had been chosen to lunch with. They seemed to sweat a lot, discreetly. The older, more assured men were like affable stone.

In every class there were women, of course. Except for an occasional recognition of a beautifully cut suit, matched to the tiny Shih-Tzu dog worn like a fur on a lady's arm, I seldom saw the international *grandes dames,* and the well-established soapmakers kept their ladies either out of town or out of their habitats, except for a few overstuffed dutiful evening meals in the quieter restaurants. The professionally ambitious Marseillais never seemed to eat in the public with

women until late at night, and then their ladies were either
outrageously dashing in their getups or comparatively prim
debutantes hoping to be engaged. Often I saw young men
alternating these rendezvous, always looking fatigued, but
still eating and drinking enough to become plump and important as soon as possible. If the women with them wore
white makeup on eyelids and lips, and leopard pants edged
with long sequin fringe, I knew they were from the hinterlands of Gstaad or Ischia and would soon move on, lean
and alert. But if they looked like prospective brides, I knew
that they would simply lose their figures, as Time and pro-
creation and digestion wore on.

Somewhere in between them and the women I saw best
and oftenest (the fishwives and waitresses and hawkers of
sugared nuts around the Old Port), there were many females
of all ages who are basically as strong and indeed invincible
as their ancestors, no matter how many generations removed.
The youngest start out in big department stores and brand-
name shoe shops and pharmacies, and they are thin and
usually lovely and as if bedazzled by life in general, and by
their own loves. They behave in a haphazard way, fitting
strange shoes, always the left foot on the right one at first,
and always three sizes too short or four sizes too wide; they
reach for aspirin on the shelf but bring down some tube of
nonprescription antibiotic; they look constantly at the nearest
clock, so as not to miss César or Patrice for a gobbled embrace
and then a sandwich. . . . (They eat a lot, always hastily.)

Older girls, still seductive, wear stern but becoming white
coats in pharmacies and delicatessens, and in little expensive
shops lined with lotions and pomades. They are the few who
have survived, it seems, and the native strain is beginning to
show, no matter how darkened their eyelids or how subtly
corseted their widening waists.

Then there are the few oddballs, the ones who stay aloof from their destinies and become night clerks in small respectable hotels, or managers of outlying branches of national banks. They are scrawny, and whether they manage a café or chandlery or a smart boutique along the Rue de Rome, they look wistful . . . discreetly tough . . . but wistful.

There are of course many trades for women in a place like Marseille, and since most of them have been practiced for centuries, there is real expertise. Competition is ruthless. I don't know what happens to the girls who fail, because of luck or health or other such hazards: probably they end in sanatoriums or cribs or gutters, or in proper warm houses filled with their own children.

But around the Vieux Port, where many of them were spawned, there are the mothers and aunts whose places they may one day seek out, the way ready salmon head upstream. They might be called "natives."

The native women of Marseille, the ones who are unmistakably of this place and no other that I have seen or read about, are short and trimly wide. As children they are thin wiry little monkeys, with large dark eyes. As girls they have a slim beauty that soon passes into what they will be for the rest of their lives, with breasts that stand up until marriage and then stay large after childbirth, without ever seeming to sag toward the ground in old age like those of taller softer females. They may develop paunches, the tidy kind that look made of steel, and among the lot of them there is never a snub nose, but instead the kind that grows stronger and beakier with time. Their arms and legs stay shapely enough, thanks surely to hard work, and their skins become like well-soaped leather, thanks perhaps to good olive oil and garlic and an occasional *pastis*, all taken by mouth in daily doses. (Tomatoes are also thanked for continuing their female vigor, according to many of their mates. . . .)

In all, the Marseillaises seem almost a part of their craggy land, like the thick trunks of the most ancient olive trees on the hills behind the city. And still they are from the sea, so that they smell of salt, and of what they eat and what they work with, but never of old sweat.

When they walk down a street, they cleave its air like small solid wooden ships driven by a mysterious inner combustion. Their men walk close alongside, often with an arm around the woman's waist or over her broad solid shoulders, pilot-fish escorting a trusted shark.

There is always the same kind of man with them, once they are mature: as short or shorter, often as stocky or else as thin as an eel. They seem to know each other as if they were born from the same egg, but there is obvious sexual enjoyment in their familiarity, and they look necessary to each other and are mutually respectful. The woman seems the more enduring of most pairs, and walks a half-step ahead, and makes decisions about things like where to sit down at what café for how long, and what to drink, and when to walk away alone so that the man can stay with other men for a time, and charge his batteries with a round of cards.

There is certainly nothing humble or timid or placating about the men. They are as male in their short strong bodies as their women are female. But they are as if pulled along in life by the dominant magnetism of their partners. They are necessary to each other, equal in their hard work, but it is plain that the woman can and often does survive several of the men whose arms lie trustingly over her shoulders as they walk together, and it is rare to see an old fisherman alone, while there are many ageless women, even shorter and broader than before, who stump strongly about, and sell fish with voices that are only a little more commanding than they were thirty years ago.

The voice of any female born and raised around the Vieux Port from countless parents of the same stock, the short dark strong breed that is a mixture of every Mediterranean race that ever touched foot there, that voice is unforgettable, once heard. It is harsh, but not hoarse, and rough and deep without being in any sense masculine. It is like the woman, built close to the earth and as strong as stone. Probably it can be soft and beautiful, in love or motherhood, but it seems bred to direct its own fate, over the sounds of storm and battle and even modern traffic. Without any doubt, a healthy fish-wife could call easily from one side of the Vieux Port to the other on a busy day, and I know one Marseillaise who sells flowers instead of fish because she lost a leg during the Oc-cupation, whose voice (and with a fine lilt to it) carries more than a block during the worst noontime bustle. (People buy flowers in Marseille much as they buy fresh sardines or bread, and noon is the time to snatch up a posy along with the loaves and fishes. . . .) Voices like hers and all her sisters' are never a shriek or shout: they are simply a part of the whole amazing strength of their bodies, basically indestruct-ible.

All this is not to say that the mature women of Marseille can be called beautiful, at least in our Western vocabulary, spoken if not felt. They have a toughness in all their attributes that is past beguilement and gentle allure. Still, they remain completely female, and therefore feminine, and while they often both outwork and outlive their partners, they seem always to be treated with a special kind of courtesy, no matter with what apparently rough bonhomie.

I have no firsthand knowledge of the private life of

heterosexual couples in the lower social and economic levels
in Marseille, any more than I do that of other more affluent
or notorious citizens, but in public there exists a patent and
perhaps strange equality among the native working class. I
have watched it for a long time, in public, along the Canebière and all around the Vieux Port.

Of course on the Quai du Port most of the females are
young. They are the chicks of the Pinball Boys, waiting im-
passively to grow out of their sleazy modish clothes, and the
figures that demand them, for the uniform of the thickened
strong bodies of the mothers, who six days a week sell fish on
the Quai des Belges and on Sundays and holidays may double
there, behind the fuming pots of sugared nuts or the little
ice-cream wagons.

On that Quai, in front of the stylish restaurants and brasseries, there are always other professional females, but they
are seldom natives. They have longer legs, and seem in flight
between the Riviera and Paris, in tourist class. I have watched
them change plumage and makeup for a long time, but they
are still for sale. In 1937, for instance, they wore the already
outdated dark suits and silver-fox scarves and petulant lips
that three or four years before were uniform in front of the
Café de la Paix in the capital, and in 1973 they were wind-
blown, without makeup, striding along the sidewalk in high
boots, flinging themselves onto *terrasse* chairs as if they had
just come from the ski runs at St. Moritz. They were the same
girls. Their older sisters, who stayed longer and, as they
tired, worked mostly around the Opera, were no more native
than they, and seemed unaware of the pert young Marseillaises hurrying along the wide sidewalks at noon and
after work, or of the mothers calling the price of sardines and
mussels resonantly on the waterfront.

Farther around the Port, on the Rive Neuve, it is more the

men's territory, although there is at least one powerful old woman there who runs her own small wholesale fish market. And I met another one, hard as basalt, who ran a café next to the Criée Publique, the wholesale auction house, a huge cave of a building, hosed out and dead-empty from perhaps nine in the morning until three or so the next, and then a wild babel of screaming buyers and sellers of the last catch, as well as of countless truckloads of fish sent fresh from Normandy and Calais and Bordeaux. (This monumental market is soon to be moved northward along the coast, toward Fos, because of the traffic problems of all the buyers and sellers on wheels. What can be the future of the ugly-beautiful structure, whose tall glassed front looks from the Port somewhat like an early railroad terminal? Empty, it echoes. Filled with yelling fish merchants it pulsates like a gigantic heart. . . .)

I had been told that the husband of the café owner next to the Criée owned a concession there, a prime position on the Port, like having a seat on the New York Stock Exchange. His wife looked powerful too, a short tough woman with that flamingly purple-red hair. When I went into their café, the boss and three men were playing cards, and she leaned over a shoulder to watch the game. There was sudden silence, neither rude nor suspicious but complete. I refused to seem abashed by it, and when the woman strolled behind the bar where I stood, I used my most acceptable accent and after the ritual exchange of *Sorry to bother—Not at all*, I asked for her help. (This is a practical beginner for all kinds of adventure, of course, and should be done with a good imitation of candor and innocence.) I was, I said truthfully, trying to find someone qualified to tell me a few facts about the fishing industry in Marseille . . . the number of commercial boats, all that.

The four men had stopped playing. I went on dauntlessly making my pitch, about how important the whole story appeared to me. The woman kept a straight face, swabbed at the impeccable zinc bar, and then asked one of the men, plainly her husband, what Madame should do. He seemed to reflect a long time in the soundless room, and finally suggested, through her, and never looking at me, that I go toward town a few doors, and ask at the ship chandler's. Another man said, his eyes firmly on his cards, "Why not the chief at the Criée?" The husband said with a mischievous grin, "This little lady would have to be there between three and six in the morning, when we work . . ." as if I never went anywhere but to Mass or bed that early. The others permitted themselves to laugh with their shoulders, in a constrained way, and looked down at their hands intently.

The woman said with some compassion, perhaps, but not smiling, "I still suggest the chandler," and I made the usual politenesses, and the minute I turned toward the door she was leaning her wildly dyed hair over her husband's shoulder and there was a healthy burst of talk and of cards slapping. It seemed to me that although she had chosen the café life, she could within an hour's notice of death or bankruptcy be back behind her piles of the day's catch, a couple of rickety folding tables away from her mother's on the Quai des Belges, and perhaps right next to her great-aunt's.

During the market hours there, men sold their catches, too, but it was the women who dominated, at least in decibels. The men simply stood behind their piles of gleaming sardines, slithery small octupi, long eels trying to get back into the dirty Port water, greyish-pink shrimps hopping within their pyramids of myriad brothers. They smiled and chatted in a detached way as they scooped the catch into newspaper cones, or whacked something into immobility for its last ride toward the kitchen, but they seemed poised for escape from all the selling end of their game. That was for the women. Once the fish got to shore, the men were set to head out to sea again . . . *les pescadous.*

Nobody seemed to protest this division of labor. The men took care of their boats, and provided as much catch as the weather and tides allowed, and sold it when their wives were birthing or grieving; the women sold what was brought in, and over the centuries had built up their own definite mannerisms of general jollity, no matter how impersonal, with now and then a clownish harsh teasing or a shouted insult, depending upon the human courtesy of the people buying their fish. In the early seventies a good gambit to amuse a circle of listeners was to tease somebody about using "Paris" or "old" francs: to an outsider accustomed to paying four francs for a batch of sardines in Bordeaux or even Aix, it was scary to have some hard-faced old biddy start screaming that she wanted four hundred, and then bawl him out, grinning all the time but ferociously, while everyone tittered a little and then drifted on along the Quai. . . .

Honorine was the typical loud canny lovable fishwife deified by Marcel Pagnol, and I have watched her for a long time. She can be mean or kind, and all the time she is shoveling the fish into newspapers, and her eyes are laughing at an inner joke. Once an Honorine sold me two Greek amphora tips that were dislodged by stormy weather from the coastal reefs, and it was the first time I ever felt that I was more than a passing gull, in every sense of the word. She was pleased that I wanted those shards, and I went off trembling with awed pleasure . . . their agelessness, hers. . . .

Around from the Quai des Belges on the Rive Neuve, for the first couple of blocks, there are some elderly tourist boats for the extra seasonal trips to the Château d'If, and a bait shack and then a lot of working fish-boats, before the dazzling yachts loom up. Land-side, there is a diminishing row of restaurants, good to pitiful and gradually being abandoned or replaced by Oriental bistros, but still rapaciously, classically, traditionally, skillfully pulling in the pedestrians. Anyone who ever planned to walk along that sidewalk, at least when I knew it from '29 to '76, was on his own, and must be strong enough to cope with what I have always called the She-Wolves, those female barkers who have for decades or perhaps centuries scared off innocents like our British visitors.

They are no doubt an offshoot of Honorine and her brood, and possibly rejects or refugees from the low-class brothels of the sea town, very typical of Marseille women in their build and their cruel ability to whisper in a harsh hiss that everybody for half a block can hear and smile about. (There is such a helpless feeling, when one of these women grabs control, that everyone within earshot of the victim feels an hysterical relief that it is not he, but another . . . so he laughs, and slides by, if he is fast on his feet.)

One or two of the Rive Neuve fishhouses in 1973 were run by darling young men who flitted around as if they were back in their hair salons, but there were still some fronted by short sardonic women, who stomped along the wet sidewalks in cheap boots in winter and half bared their firm broad bodies in summer, and performed everything but a half-Nelson to grab a client before he reached the next restaurant.

"Come in, honey, come in *here*," they would command roughly, with ancient practiced blackmail and all the evil seduction of bad tides and rough weather in their voices. They would mutter in a hoarse provocative voice as loud as a shout, "Take a look, sweetheart! One look at that display, and you'll bring your little darling right in! Look at that lobster, a female busting with eggs! Look at those pink shrimps standing straight up! Hey, now, don't miss this chance!"

A lot of people were so dazed and embarrassed by this attack that they shuffled into the dens like helpless sheep. Some simply knew where they were going and ignored or smiled at the tireless hustlers, and sailed past. A few listened seriously, peered in at what the customers were gobbling, read the posted menus again, and either went in under their own steam or did not.

My sister Norah and I soon got to know where we wanted to eat, and how to cope with the vocal hazards of getting there, and the She-Wolves recognized this with forgiving fatalism and a friendly shrug.

There was one small older one, with frankly greying hair instead of the usual purple-red and with an oddly school-marmish air about her. Perhaps I liked her for this, and perhaps because she worked in front of an obviously second-rate place and had almost none of the brashness of her colleagues. Once Norah said to me with some disapproval or surprise, "You patted her on the shoulder when you said 'No,'" and I said, "But the last time she patted *me*! On the arm! That time I said, 'Not *tonight*.' And it went off all right. It seemed like a logical answer."

That grey-haired one was the She-Wolf I had promised to return to, never having gone to her place at all. For vague reasons I had felt shy and awkward at her advances, as if she were my second-grade teacher, and "I swear we'll come," I said, smiling, raising a hand solemnly. She remembered, and would give me a private twinkle, the next time I'd say, before she could begin her pitch, "It's still a promise. . . ." Then one night we took some visitors along the quay and headed right for her place, to keep my word at last, but in a

pure funk went to the restaurant just before hers, because the
array of harridans out soliciting for patrons of bouillabaisse
on that weekend was too unnerving for our present guests.

When we came out, several bowls and bottles later, the
smaller thinner older woman was a few paces down the block,
still conning possible customers, and she gave me a sad look,
and we never really touched each other again. She knew
where we had been, and perhaps why, but she remembered
the pact. . . .

Some people think these are bad women, whores. Certainly
they are an embarrassment to proper Anglo-Saxons who have
never before been so openly and noisily offered wares which
in this case are gastronomical instead of sexual, and perhaps
many of them spend their few free hours in much their accustomed rhythm, horizontally instead of on their sturdy
feet. But, wolves that they have become or may always have
been, I feel an almost affectionate admiration for them.

(A typical American appraisal I thus am happy to contra-
dict is a nationally syndicated newspaper "feature": ". . . old
women stand like prostitutes in front of the area's numer-
ous restaurants, hustling customers for seafood of dubious
quality.")

It certainly *looks* as if these Fallen Women solicit, although I have never been so blatantly treated by the many
whores I have met on the sidewalks of my life. But along the
seafood street in Marseille they are not really old. Of course
they are not built like California carhops or International
Bunnies, because they seem to have been born and bred for
more than two thousand years around the Vieux Port, but
mostly they are very vital and female, looking exactly as
they have looked for all that time, short and a little thick,
with faces carved from olivewood. It is hard to judge women

chronologically when history itself is involved, in Marseille as in Peking, but I would put the average age of the procuresses along Bouillabaisse Row at about forty-four.

While I am protecting them from something they would never even bother to sniff at, their image in Western eyes, I must protest again: the seafood offered along their two or three blocks of the Rive Neuve should not be classed as "dubious." It is often mediocre, but that is the fault of the kitchen rather than of the fish, which cannot be anything but fresh, because the wretched pantries behind the dining rooms have little modern equipment for chilling or freezing. A whiff of spoiled fish on the Rive Neuve would kill the reputation of even a poor place in ten minutes, because most of the people who eat along there are natives, in spite of the seeming predominance of tourists. Some of the small restaurants have excellent chefs, or chefs skilled in soups or deep-fries or a dozen other adjuncts of fish cookery itself, and the Marseillais know about that, and the tourist is simply lucky. Some places have tired cooks, or even tired fry-kettles, but never tired fish. . . .

As I have said before, a few people (mostly Saxon) are not used to being stared at as they sit in a bare bright window sucking at shells and claws, while on the other side of the glass people stroll past them on the Rive Neuve and look at what is left on their plates, and then at the menu posted at the door, to see if it seems worth the price, and then either shrug off the She-Wolves or a little sheepishly come into the place they like the looks of. Americans are fascinated and rather tittery about this direct approach. English people find it too embarrassing for real comfort. Swiss, Germans, Scandinavians seem to like it, because it is "foreign" and relaxed. Italians find it "natural"; where there is fresh fish there is good food.

No doubt there are bad days, in any of the understaffed badly housed seafood restaurants along the Rive Neuve, just as there may be some "bad women" in the assortment of sidewalk touts and harpies. But who needs to eat an expensive touristic bouillabaisse when there are a dozen kinds of shellfish lying on green weeds waiting to be shelled, all gently breathing in and out, and several kinds of swimmers doomed to the poach pan or the skillet?

In one window of every fishhouse along the quay there is a tilted display, fresh once and sometimes twice a day, of the prettiest catch. The former hairdressers make the most whimsical, but in the plainest little restaurant there may be a curled fish balancing a giant shrimp on his nose, in a bed of silver sardines, with one lobster waving a feeler feebly behind him, to prove the possible class of the place. Norah and I liked to walk into town early, or at least by ten in the morning, to go to the Flower Market at the top of the Canebière, and we would see bleary waiters and some of the She-Wolves fabricating these fishy set pieces. The "girls" might be in curlers or with old sweaters over their nightgowns. The "boys" would be black-chinned and tousled. All their foreheads were wrinkled with concentration, and their lips pursed, as they tried the purple of a pile of sea urchins against the hideous fangy grey-pink of a *rascasse*, and then shook their heads and moved onto the set a majestic goblet hung with pink prawns. . . . Now and then we would be spotted, and there was always a smile and nod, and of course a beckoning suggestive leer from the females to get us back for lunch or dinner. . . .

There were many other fish places in Marseille, more elgant and often much better. But none of them had those fantastic women. They were not the same: they seemed tamer. The truth is, I suspect, that no man in the world would ever

have the gall to behave as those females did and do along the
Rive Neuve. Inside their dens, their caves, there were male
waiters, of course, and men to help open the endless orders
of shellfish from a banked dripping table or a great counter,
but it was the other sex that dominated. I admit to being
cowed by them at times, and to skulking along on the other
side of the quay with my head turned away from their stern
beady eyes, but at the same time I can still feed on an intrinsic
courage that emanated from them, and may do so forever.

I I

Like every other *cours* in Provence, and like every such gathering place in most towns there around the Mediterranean, but
especially in Marseille, the Cours Belsunce is unique. There
can be no other like it, just as there can be no other Piazza
di San Marco, although there are other formidably beautiful
"squares" in Italy.

Belsunce is a wide street, tree-shaded in summer on the
east side; the western side toward the sea was fairly
thoroughly destroyed in the bombardment of May 27, 1944,
and is now being filled in with high-rise 'scrapers. A few
good old houses still stand, back of Belsunce, to prove its
former dignity, and to the north it teems with life that can
never be alien to a place like Marseille, although it is by
now an "Arab Quarter," and has always had a shabby reputation among the more comfortably housed citizens of this
ancient cosmopolis.

It was built in 1666 because the citizens were jealous of the
beautiful Cours Mirabeau in Aix, their purportedly cultural
and political rival. It was the style then to *stroll*, now a lost
art: rich people showing their latest fashions at certain

hours, and nodding chattily to their favored peers; poorer people doing what poor people did in those and any days, shoving and eating and laughing, and showing their various inward and outer sores and joys, like all the others.

Belsunce, called *Cours de Marseille* in proud defiance of the promenade in Aix, was opened in 1670, by decree of Louis XIV. First it was planted with a tree whose name I cannot find, *micocouliers*. I assume it was fast-growing, since the Cours was an immediate center of the town, and had only been a-building for four years. Then there were mulberry trees, those marvels of cool shade and messy pathways. In 1750, though, the *allées* along both sides of the Cours were replanted with elms, and some ninety years later with plane trees, many of which still stand nobly along the wide meeting-street, as they do on the envied Cours Mirabeau in Aix, even more beautifully.

Plane trees need a lot of root water (in Aix they are said to survive on the buried canal that once flowed where the Cours now stands) and there was plenty on the Cours de Marseille. Halfway up it from what is now the Canebière there was a great fountain, the Medusa, spouting from fifty mouths, and in 1726 two more fine drinking troughs were built for man and beast, with two more Medusas spitting out unfailing streams of cool water to both sides.

These Medusas made a division, more aesthetic than some, between the high and low classes of the town. On the north side of the biggest fountain, life was rough, and inevitably its verities spilled down toward the richer world, so that the art of pocket-picking gave the whole Cours a bad reputation by 1722, and few of the elegants dared set foot on it after dark. It was still called "the loveliest spot in Europe," though, just as the rival Cours Mirabeau is still called "the most beautiful Main Street in the world." And while toward the north the common people teemed and roistered, south of the Medusa, always spouting "a prodigious quantity of water," according to current chronicles, the Cours Belsunce was "elegant and animated . . . the rendez-vous of handsome personnages in embroidered clothes, their opera hats folded under one arm, their swords flapping against their haunches . . . the ladies made a fashion-show of their newest gowns, following every inconsistency of the changing styles, and the god of Vanity received there on the Grand Cours his most expensive compliments."

Aix has managed to hold on to its five lively fountains along the middle of its lovely street, in spite of wars, traffic, and other disasters. In contrast, in Marseille the great central fountain was knocked down before many years because it was believed to hinder the horse-drawn circulation to and from Aix and points north! The two smaller Medusas continued to fill the marble watering troughs, however, until 1841, when they were judged to be "too countrified," and were replaced by ugly cast-iron watering basins. (One of these was found in a pit in 1955, and is now exhibited in the Borély Museum, to hell-and-gone south of the city. It is a monument to Progress, at least . . . but hardly an archaeological treasure.)

In 1853 a bronze statue of Monseigneur François Xavier de Belsunce de Castelmoron, former bishop and one of the most devoted workers in Marseille during the horrible plague of 1720, was formally if belatedly erected at the top of the wide promenade, which from then on has been named for him, instead of being simply another small-town Provençal "cours." And once more traffic got the best of civic pride, and the noble old man was moved to the front of the Bishop's Palace, now Police Headquarters. During the last active war the statue somehow escaped being melted down for German armaments, and made another move, to stand in front of the

Cathedral, La Major, which is perhaps less lasting in its hideous neo-Byzantine bulk than the innate elegance of the warrior who fought to save his city from death by the pox. It is hard to conceive that the traffic of cars-buses-trucks will push him once more off his pedestal, as it did the Medusas finally, but an expression of clear resignation is intrinsic to the good bishop's face.

Traffic itself is as intrinsic, of course, to the Cours Belsunce today. But the sidewalk, at least on the east side, is as wide as it once was, and in summer the generous plane trees still shade it. And people drift along it in the special and very intense fashion true to any such place, from the Galería in Milan to the Plaza in Chapala. They are going someplace, maybe, and maybe coming from someplace, at a special speed that cannot be judged by its apparent indolence. Perhaps they do not really know the wheres and whences, much less the whys, but there is a latent purposefulness in the way they move, and in the looks they give to the foodstuffs in the sidewalk stands, to the windows of the little shops, to the other people sitting in the cafés, waiting for them or for somebody like them.

Did the hard division between two social worlds happen when the great spouting fountain went down? Was it really demolished to make the rich safer from the street thieves who lived on the wrong side of the Medusa watering troughs, rather than to ease traffic onto the long road to Aix? (One contemporary wrote that the whole Cours had "a very bad reputation, complete with exotic bazaars and 'Levantines'!") Whatever the reasons, Belsunce is by now a conglomerate, a puzzle, which can possibly be called, if not solved, a potential melting pot. There are few visible signs, except for an occasional doorway or cornice, of the affluent politicians and noblemen who once showed off their silks and their

sweethearts and even built their townhouses on the "right"
side of the fountain, and the commoners who used to stay
up toward the Porte d'Aix now own the whole wide street, off
the Canebière. And the minute anyone steps onto the Cours,
a special lifebeat starts, that has been there, shunned sometimes, feared sometimes, for a few hundred years, through
various historical throes and spasms and cultural and archi-
tectural upheavals, all felt instinctively but perhaps unre-
membered except for the bombardments of 1944, whose scars
still show.

Cafés sprawl onto the wide east sidewalk, always looking
half-filled with slender dark men hunched over tiny cups of
coffee or glasses of pale tea or violently orange soda. They
talk in groups of two or three, never loudly, or sit alone with
an expectant patience. Shapeless ageless women hurry up to
the narrow streets of the Arab quarter with heavy string
bags of provisions from the main open market on the other
side of the Canebière. There are dogs, and children, and
surprisingly few identifiable whores. ("Arabs" have their
own prides and prejudices.) The dogs and the children seem
to know what they are there for: to wait for their masters or,
on Sundays, to work in the booths, according to the number
of legs they may be endowed with.

Along that east side of Belsunce there are all kinds of
stands: food mostly, hot-cold-spiced-sweet, and then souvenirs
of Marseille to send back to North Africa; cheap small rugs
made in USA; trays of watches and ballpoint pens and bright
jeweled combs. The smells are good, in the ever-fresh air
under the plane trees. There is very little jukebox din, as on
the Quai du Port on weekends, but there seems no wish or
need to play the Levantine or Algerian music that would be
expected from the looks of most of the people on the Cours,

and that is wailed out elsewhere in Marseille, even a block or two northward, off the Rue d'Aix.

When I have been in town, I have always gone to Belsunce, and have retained to a probably unflattering degree my invisibility. Women are nonexistent there, as such, except for the ancient drudges with their market bags and their soft long shapeless dresses and one tattoo between the downcast eyes. They are as shadowy as I, to the quiet throngs of men who move idly, like tidal waters, along the Cours and then off narrow streets like Présentines, Ste. Barbe, Chapeliers. Eastward, on the Grands Rue, little open shops spill piles of clothes onto the sidewalks, and more clothes hang like flocks of garish birds on high hangers, and the merchants lounge against mounds of rugs and bolted yardage, or squat philosophically on piles of repossessed overcoats and work clothes. As everywhere in Marseille, rich or poor, an astonishing number of shoes are for sale, cheap or costly and obviously expendable. In the Arab Quarter they are cheap, and as available as a glass of tea. If there is any of the haggling that Westerners expect in Eastern bazaars, it is low-keyed, and the voices are more a steady murmur than anything excited, except perhaps during a period of anger or political revolt. I would not know except from the daily papers, because I have always walked these streets in times of seeming easiness, and in daylight.

Even the poorest shops in this quarter have a few traditional robes and coverings hanging in them, to beautify young girls and brides and I assume all women, except the oldest ones with string bags. Up past the Cours on the Rue d'Aix there are a few comparatively elegant stores, with windows filled with exotic exquisite long coats, and swatches of gold-shot silk, and jeweled slippers.

Nowhere are there women. Even the ancient biddies disappear, once they have crossed the Canebière and gone silently up Belsunce. The men, then, must be the ones who buy such beauty for their brides, their nubile daughters. . . .

Once only, though, I saw an amazing female in the Quarter.

At the top of the Cours there is a junky-looking store, like many in San Francisco's Chinatown: one knows instinctively that at the back, behind all the gaudy trash, there will be some rare porcelain, yellowed ivory, an amber hairpin. . . . I was considering an embroidered collar of gold thread and bits of turquoise, and to cool my greedy wits before a definite and perhaps predestined extravagance I went eastward for a few paces, on the Rue St. Jean, I think. The shopkeeper looked fatalistically after me, sure I would return to his bait.

The woman coming toward me cut through the tide of men like a shining blade. They fell back from her with a discreet but obvious awareness, quite different from their acceptance of my invisibility. They did not seem to look at her, or at each other behind her, but they *saw* her. Perhaps they knew her, or what she was.

She was unusually tall, surely a German or Swede, with a pale broad face. It had either seven or nine symmetrically designed tattoos or perhaps paintings on it, in a pale blue that was clearly outlined on the white skin, even though her whole face looked as if dusted with powder or flour. Her blue eyes were narrowed, fixed on an inner goal and looking only toward it. She wore a kind of pillbox on her head, with straight blond hair pulled tightly up into it, and pale blue gauzy veils fell from it, over all of her long and perhaps slender body except her impassive face.

She glanced fleetingly at me, or rather her eyes touched me as if I were one more object within her immediate view, and then she sailed past, with the silks fluttering in her wake.

A Considerably Tan

Book Alley

INV

611 E. Colorado Blvd., Pasadena, CA 91101 U.S.A.
(626) 683-8083   Toll Free: (888) 457-1899   FAX (626) 683-8084

Name _____ Phone	
Address _____	
City _____ State/Z	

SOLD BY	CASH

ITEM	DESCRIPTION
	A Considerable To~~
	EXCHANGE OR STORE CREDIT WITH RECEIPT ONLY

I was astounded by her, and wondered almost fearfully why she was abroad, on a bright crowded Sunday, when all the other women of the quarter remained hidden behind tight shutters. She seemed to be walking straight toward something, and while nobody stepped aside, it was a ridiculous impossibility that anyone could or would be in her way.

I went back to the corner shop almost unsteadily, my eyes still on the strange blue markings of that exalted face, on the implacable progress of that tall body through the crowds of quiet dark men. The collar of gold thread and turquoise looked vulgar to me, and it cost too much, and the shopkeeper shrugged smilingly and said he would see me again some day, which he did.

And I walked down the Cours Belsunce, past all the little cafés and foodstalls and snack bars with windows full of unbelievably sweet oily cookies painted in wild pinks and yellows, and my mind was full of puzzlement. What kind of woman had I seen? She was regally beyond evil, and perhaps good. She could have controlled all the prostitution or heroin market in the Mediterranean world, or she could have been the adaptive and charitable refugee wife of a local Arab peddler, but she was perhaps the most impassive *force* I had ever seen in a female, and the most mysterious, even in Marseille. She must have existed long before the Cours was built, long before the Phoceans came; A.D. 1670, 600 B.C., such trivia fade fast when someone, something like that, walks along its own private path.

I I I

There is an iron staircase, a steep long footbridge that goes straight down to the Rive Neuve of the Old Port in Marseille, from very high up, near the ancient Abbey of St. Victor. It spans what used to be the Canal de Rive Neuve, that bypassed the Port and hopefully drained off not only some of the shipping but much of the pollution that a couple of hundred years ago made the city one of the world's prime stinkholes. The canal is now dry, and used mostly to store construction equipment for the gradual rebuilding of some of the quays. It is ugly to look down upon, but sometimes one does, especially on the upward climb of the stairs. I usually did, to catch my breath, and, once I was sure of the drabness below me, I looked instead at the old church, or into the star-shaped ramparts of the Fort St. Nicolas beyond it. They calmed my lurking vertigo.

One day I had stopped halfway up the hideous resounding stairs, and then started on the second half of the climb, when an elderly lady, very nicely dressed in the discreet well-cut black clothes and artful "toque" that are worn only by French women of her age and station (She is on the Ladies' Board of St. Victor, I said to myself, and is a member of the musical committee for the Bach concerts . . .), started down the top steps and then faltered when she saw me.

Lady, I said to myself, this is no place to hesitate . . . either keep moving, or sit down until you feel better. I kept on climbing slowly, and she came down, holding onto the cold metal rail. When she got about five steps from me, she smiled archly and said in a fluty voice, the kind ladies of her age and station reserve for waitresses in tea shops or their own grandchildren, "It is so difficult, in fact it is impossible, to know whether one is walking toward a man or a woman these days!" She laughed musically. We both stopped going down and up, after this strange unsolicited comment, and finally I said, with some stiffness I suppose, "I assure you, Madame, that in spite of my pants suit I am a female."

The whole thing suddenly seemed almost unbelievable, out of control, a dream, as we stood there on the ugly iron footbridge with the dead canal far below us and piles of gravel and rusting cement mixers, and the clean air blowing in from the sea. She laughed, this time with a little less musical certainty, and said with some confusion, "Things do seem mixed up, don't they? Girls act like men, and it is rumored that men even act like . . . well, not like real men . . . sometimes. Here in Marseille all kinds of strange things seem to happen, like seeing a man come up the stairs and then it is not a man at all. But of course I know you don't mean to look like a man. That is—"

I interrupted her, and I knew that soon I would regret being rude, but for the moment I *felt* rude. I felt affronted by this silly ladylike simpering relic, tottering toward me down the dreadful iron stairs. "No, Madame," I said very distinctly, "I do not mean to look like a man. I am not a man. I am a traveller, and I find a pants suit excellent on trains and buses and planes and even iron footbridges."

She looked increasingly flustered, as for a moment or two I really wanted her to, because I was temporarily past pity or empathy. I thought her first simpering remark was un-called for, especially on a hideous high arch that, at best, is some kind of atavistic challenge to my steadiness and cour-age. "You are a foreigner," she said triumphantly, as if she had found a toehold in our encounter.

"Yes, I am. I am from California," I said to beat her to asking me.

"Ah, what an enormous country," she exclaimed exactly as I knew she would, loosing her gloved grip on the rail long enough to put her hand over her heart.

"Yes," I said, and then I cruelly went on in the ritual I had learned too well from many of her counterparts over the teacups in Dijon and points south, east, and north in France for the past forty years. "The United States are much too large and enormous, and we are a very young nation, still feeling growing pains, not knowing our strength, making all kinds of blunders that must be blamed on a spiritual adolescence. We are a mixture of the most daring refugees from every oldest country of the world. We are an amalgam. Our thinking and even our everyday manners are impulsive, and often crude."

She blinked at me, and then said with new firmness, "But you speak quite coherently." She sounded polite but astonished, and this made me even more impatient, mostly because I hated to stand there on that bridge, far above the cruel sand of the old canal, with the wind nudging us. I bowed and said, "Thank you."

She smiled in a flustered way, and said, "Well, I must say goodbye. You are wearing a costume that I cannot accustom myself to, but one can tell that you are obviously nicely brought up. Goodbye, goodbye."

I bowed again to her, and listened to her careful steps down to the bottom of the footbridge. Then I went stamping up to the top of the iron stairs, and almost immediately felt swamped with remorse at having been rude, and to an older woman. How could I have sounded so cold and basically so irritated by this harmless sweetfaced lady? On the other hand, how had she dared simply announce to me that she could not tell whether I was male or female? What business was it of hers? But perhaps she had just been given a mood changer, a tranquilizer of some kind? Perhaps her daughter had just died of cancer and she had been to St. Victor to pray? Certainly she had quit her accustomed role as a well-bred aging lady to whinny to me, as I panted up the iron steps toward her. Had it been because she needed to talk to

another human being? Then why had she said such a strange
thing? And after all, what business *was* it of hers? I had
said nothing about her peculiarly traditional black costume
with the little toque and the smooth kid gloves, and the
handbag for her rosary.

I tried not to think of her faded face with the small good
bones underneath the skin, and her puzzled eyes. I felt
acutely, painfully, ashamed of myself for a few more minutes, and now and then I still do, and probably always will,
for not having recognized a call, perhaps a call for help, from
another dizzied human.

Chapter 5

ONE OF THE MEN

In 1973, while my sister Norah was wandering through the dusty stacks of small but famous Marseille libraries, public and private, on the trail of Mary Magdalen's lesser-known apocrypha, I spent most of my time absorbing the general aspect of the Old Port, either from our two big windows above the Rive Neuve or down on the waterfront. I was largely silent. Opening a conversation there can be either provocative or impolitic, depending upon where it is done, and I chose to remain inaudible and thus somewhat unseen. I have been fairly conditioned, though, to love to talk, perhaps especially in French, and that is why it was good for me to meet the doctor down our street.

Norah disliked him immediately, for several reasons including the fact that he had something like fourteen children, and was therefore a selfish Catholic (she occasionally sounds oddly like her Irish grandmother!), and also because sometimes I would go to report to him on basic matters such as how one of his pills was performing, and instead of being back at the apartment in half an hour, I would come in three hours later, my head humming with his well-educated volubility. I was tiddly on his good talk, like a child drunk on fruit juice after too long a thirst.

My sister, naturally more anxious about why a pill was necessary than what possible effect it might have, took out her uneasiness by being coldly disapproving of my lackadaisical manner, and indirectly of my sparkle. I told her Dr. Gabillaud was talkative. "Plain gabby!" she said. And he is still Gabby Gabillaud, high on my list of therapeutic spellbinders. I would like to see him again. I feel averse, though, to taking up a doctor's time unless I need his trained help, and three years after I swallowed the man's capsules in Marseille, when I returned there, I could neither cough nor creak commendably enough to ring his doorbell.

I think often of him, as I do of a few other medicos in France and Switzerland and England, and it both interests and saddens me that with them I feel a stronger bond than I do with their peers in my own country. This is not because I was a foreigner, thus calling out their extra compassion, their fleeting amiability. On the contrary, I was probably an interruption in their familiar rounds of office and house calls, and obviously a transient and unprofitable investment in the kind of energy that a good doctor spends beyond his professional obligations.

And Gabby Gabillaud and some of those other Europeans did spend it on me. It was more valuable to my adrenalin supply, my loyally pumping heart, my occasional aches and quakes, than any injections or suppositories yet devised. When they had finished their explorations, both verbal and manual, and scribbled their lingua franca prescriptions for what may or may not have ailed me, they would sit back with a small sigh, look at me as if I had suddenly come into focus as a person and not a problem, and begin to talk, about Paul Valéry, or German-Swiss dumplings, or a former student of Maillol who had just fallen off her unfinished statue of a ninety-foot phallus. I would respond like the proverbial old firehorse to the whiff of conversational smoke. I would feel younger, more like a human being. And when the unknown man sitting with apparent enjoyment behind his desk looked suddenly at his watch, I would stand up as if I must leave a good dinner before its end, and walk out in a heady cloud of silly jokes and puns, epigrams, criticisms, all playing like firelight over *language*, language used as it should be used: a prime means of communication.

Gabby talked that way. Sometimes I wondered cynically if he really did, or if he merely sounded fine because I was so hungry for French from somebody besides a Marseille waiter or cabdriver, but by now I know that he was an intelligent, well-educated man, and that *he* needed to talk to *me*. What is more, he let me talk too, and I heard my rusty accent grow smoother, and felt my mind stretch. I asked him questions, sensing that he wanted me to. He would rise like a wily old trout, recognizing my bait, and knowing how to escape it with a flick and a neat flash.

Once I heard someone come into his untended waiting room and begin to walk around, sigh, drop a magazine. I finally said something polite about not staying. He glanced at his schedule on his big flat desk, said, "That's old Fantoni. He's in for his shot. He'll be all right for a while," and went right on about the need for men in high office to have their own escape hatches. He told me graphically about a schoolmate of his, now a famous political leader, who since puberty has hidden at regular times to listen day and night to recorded music. "It's like periodic alcoholism," I said. "Yes, but this is restorative, not destructive," Gabby said. "And by now, it

is a double game with him. It works up his glands to fool
the journalists, who link him with international starlets,
secret rendezvous with nuclear-physicists. Even his wife be-
lieves that he has at least one mistress. He comes back from
the three days of Baroque music, or 1930s jazz, a renewed
man."

In the waiting room, Fantoni banged open a window, and
groaned a little. I stood up again. "Doctor, do you wish to
see me next week?" He looked as if he was trying to remember why I was there, and then permitted himself a small
grin as he bowed perfunctorily to me. "Of course," he said.
"Monday at eleven, when the office is not so crowded."

Old Fantoni, the only other soul around, looked crosswise
at me, and held his stomach gently with one hand. I felt
sheepish but exhilarated; Norah would be chilly with me,
and nobody would notice how much better my French
sounded, and I wondered why this did not happen at home.
Why could not my wits, if not my American accent, be
sharpened by my monthly visit to a trusted friend's office?
Why would I come out feeling as dull as when I went in?
I would have an impression of the doctor's real fatigue, of
being rushed through a hideously crowded schedule, of needing more than the routine checks of pulse, blood pressure,
respiration. I needed to have more than my prescriptions renewed. And what was perhaps most tonic of all in my visits
to Gabby and his French peers was that in some ways I felt
that I too had been good medicine. . . .

Maybe our doctors at home, I thought as I headed for the
apartment above the Vieux Port, are so overcrowded and
harried that they cannot permit themselves to be more than
healers to their patients. They choose, in self-survival, to have
little sustained contact with the sick, in their training and
then in the clinics and huge hospitals and busy groups they

graduate to. Now and then a handful will break away, to try in an idealistic fashion to recapture the old spirit of "the country doctor" in a rural community. They must learn to make house calls, and to drive into the hills in storms to deliver babies. They must think about their own children's chancy schooling and about their frustrated bored wives. They must make annual contact with "the outside," at some exhausting medical conference, and try not to listen to their classmates wondering how to cope with income taxes, nor to the blandishments of great pharmaceutical laboratories, nor to their in-laws suggesting they give up this person-to-person nonsense and specialize in ophthalmology or psychopodiatry, in an affluent suburb where they will, first thing, put in swimming pool and tennis court. . . .

I wondered how French or English or Swiss G.P.s found the nerve to avoid all this pressure. How did they raise fourteen children? How did they keep their wives? The first time I saw Gabby, for instance, he came to our lower-class, shabby flat at almost ten at night, after his rounds. He had been called at perhaps five o'clock by our concierge, who "went" to him for some female trouble but knew he would cure my wild coughing. He looked like a tired, quiet, middle-aged businessman. He listened to my story, gave me about six prescriptions to be filled the next day, did nothing about immediate relief of what I felt was a cosmic whoop, and stood up as if he would like to dust off his trousers. When I asked him his fee, he said, "Two thousand francs." I was horrified until I realized that he was pre-de Gaulle and meant twenty, and he put the bills, worth about four dollars, into his coat pocket, and asked me to see him in three days.

I cannot remember any late house calls before in my lives in Europe, nor do I remember paying money to a doctor. They would send a bill annually, after I had forgotten that on August 4 the younger girl had thrown up after a bee sting and that on November 29 the older had gashed her leg in an awkward slalom. . . . But Gabillaud lived in a blue-collar part of the quarter, and perhaps it was easier that way. Certainly the fee did not seem to interest him one way or another. I thought he was a cold fish, and felt peevish that he had not left some magical pill to make me stop coughing.

Three days and two shots later (given by a licensed nurse sent from the neighborhood pharmacy where I had all the prescriptions filled), I went a couple of blocks down our ugly street to his apartment house. His office was on the ground floor, and he lived on the one above, according to the mailboxes. The waiting room was grim and dark, perhaps a former mean, measly dining room. There was an inadequate but elegant desk in the little hallway, with a telephone, and I learned later that one or another of the doctor's attractive daughters occasionally marked appointments there. A half-open door showed the former kitchen, now with an examination table crowded into it. Then Gabby opened the final door, and I went into a room that in a flash reminded me of other forgotten doctors' offices: London, Berne, Dijon, all completely different from the professional cubbyholes at home, so antiseptic and impersonal.

It was big, once the *salon* of the apartment, with tall windows opening onto a neglected green garden, shabby and tranquil. There were good armchairs and a chaise longue and plenty of books and reading lights, and there was a general feeling that the family used the room whenever it was not a hospice for the dying and the sickly. It felt clean, healthy, and receptive. I sank into a fine chair upholstered in worn silk, and forgot to cough.

The doctor looked freshly shaved, and almost dapper, compared with the rumpled man of the night call. I deduced, early in our game, that he was hipped on allergies: he started out by tracing my chronic bronchial cough to a life-long predilection for living near the sea, the ocean, even lakes and ponds. His logical questions proved him right, at least to himself. Then he used his own case to strengthen mine, and bared his weak defenses in unwitting betrayal.

His whole career, his life in Algeria as head surgeon in a big civil hospital after years of study and practice in Bordeaux and Paris, had ended abruptly, tragically: he told me that in 1961, during the Mutiny, he had developed a violent reaction to *rubber*. "Had this ever happened before?" I asked with guileful innocence, thinking of that time of wild revolt and of the thousands of people fleeing Algeria and of all the scandal and anguish there and in France. "No," he said, almost serenely. "Within a few days it became obvious that never again could I wear rubber gloves. And that meant giving up surgery forever. It meant leaving a country I loved, abandoning my patients, uprooting my children from their schools. An allergy, Madame . . . a simple twist in the metabolic pattern, the body chemistry of a mature man! I was finished!"

He tried to use this sad story as a proof that once back in California I must undergo a long series of tests to decide what it was about sea air that made me cough. I pretended to consider all this seriously for the next few months, but his apparent unwillingness to track down his own sudden inability to tolerate rubber gloves seemed quizzical to me, and I sniffed out what I could of his neurotic nature.

I noticed that his hands were strong and firm-skinned, but that he held a pen as if it hurt him. He touched doorknobs with care. He never shook hands, as so many people do in southern France. Once he decided to examine some of my

orifices in the converted kitchen. To do it he rinsed his hands
from a bottle and put on mittens of thin clear plastic; afterward he washed his hands very gently with two kinds of soap,
powdered them, and ran a sterilized orangewood stick under
his nails and around the cuticle, in a slow preoccupied way.
When he saw me watching him, he asked me curtly to wait
for him in his office, but when he came in he did not seem
anything but bland and interested in me-the-patient.

Over the next weeks I asked him questions that were so
obvious as to make me feel ridiculous: were allergic condi-
tions slow in building; was there any proven connection between them and emotional stress; could they be cured or
merely alleviated, with the possible causes and cures dictated
by chemistry or by circumstance? The doctor never seemed
aware of my game: I was a "case" to him, and he himself
was *not*. He was an extraordinary example of the quirkiness
of Fate, or Providence, or perhaps God. People like me could
have series of injections in their bottoms, or move to a new
climate, or stop eating eggs. He was a surgeon cut down in
his prime, a victim of the sudden curse of wearing rubber
gloves. There was no remedy for any punishment as unique
as his. He shrugged, laid his strong, somewhat hairy hands
on his desk as if they were made of porcelain, and went into
another casual story about his famous schoolmate who played
records instead of having a mistress, or about a former patient
who raised cheetahs (Gabby was given one every New Year,
and sent it to the Longchamps zoo), or the rise in heroin addiction in Western Europe. . . .

He talked with somewhat the same self-enjoyment, somewhat the sensuality he showed in cleaning his nails, but
with more animation. We both enjoyed it. I talked too (another vocal voluptuary!), and he seemed to enjoy what I

asked and occasionally stated. Once he lost his usual ironical detachment, when we were talking about the way young people, his in Marseille and mine in Pittsburgh or Berkeley, young people anywhere, can be pushed into drug abuse. He turned very pale, and said, "I have spent my life learning how to save lives, and I am ready to die to oppose capital punishment, but I am also ready to kill anyone who sells drugs. *Kill!*" He forgot his hands, and raised them to make a violent gesture of pressing them unto death around a throat. . . .

And only once did he permit himself to touch me except professionally. That was the day after I fell on my face, when he put one hand for a minute on my shoulder, as if in his concern he must silently pat me, commend me, encourage me.

And that was the Monday after Palm Sunday, which is a special holiday in France and perhaps most so in Marseille. It is almost the end of Lent, almost spring. People swarm out of their nests like lustful bees, helpless lemmings, and walk or ride into the countryside. If they own cars, they throw grandparents and children into the back, and drive as fast as they can along the nearest and preferably the most crowded highways. They head, afoot or on wheels, for good food and open air, preferably with a view thrown in.

My sister and I felt the fever of Palm Sunday along with countless other Marseillais, and after a remarkably good lunch up on the Rue des Catalans we started the interminable trek on the curving Corniche J. F. Kennedy, which is very wide, very ugly, built along the wild coast outside the city. To our left were six lanes of cars full of people going anywhere as fast as possible. To our right was the Mediterranean, looking pale blue except on the surly rocks below the high cement curve of the roadway. We began to trudge instead of walk. Finally we sighted a little café across the way, and far from coincidentally it was located by one of the rare stop-and-go lights. We decided to cross and sit down.

We grabbed a green light, ran to the pedestrian island just as the yellow went on, and unlike us in every way except on Palm Sunday, 1973, we decided to run for the curb before the red went on.

The island was shaped somewhat like a badly designed throat lozenge, larger at one end, and sloping on the six-inch sides, and I misjudged by about an inch, and instead of taking one hurried step across the little raised platform, I plunged off it, straight forward, five feet and seven-plus inches, into the path of the nearest of three lanes of happy carefree well-fed celebrants getting up speed again as fast as possible with their green light.

I heard Norah cry "*Oh!*" and felt her pull me back onto the soft warm welcoming asphalt of the pedestrian island, where I would have liked to take a long nap. But there was a general screech of brakes, and a dozen people slowed and called out, "Can we help? Do you need help? Can we take her to a doctor?" "No, no, thank you," Norah called back, and she began to look at my face, while the motorists gathered new speed. Then two young men ran from the sea edge of the Corniche, and bent over me. They were interns at Ste. Marguerite, they said to my sister, and one picked up my face from its lovely cushion and said, "Hospital. Now," and the other ran back (Norah said he simply waltzed between the long lanes of traffic), and wheeled their car around toward the café we'd been heading for.

"Can she walk?" "Yes, she can," and I was mopping off my face with wet paper towels the barman brought me in the toilet. People looked compassionately at me as I drifted in and out of the café, but there was no disgust at my ugliness, my bloodied clothes.

Outside, the two young men folded me into the back of a ratty old *deux-cheveaux* with its cloth top down. The older more decisive one sat beside me looking as wary as a pointing setter, with one hand on my wrist. I said, reorganizing my mind and mouth to be polite or at least conscious, "This is a boring way for you to celebrate Palm Sunday," and he said, "Oh, we were just cruising. Nice sun today."

We drove a long time, I thought, and then were in a huge collection of grubby old buildings and half-finished sidewalks, and I was in Emergency Surgery while Norah thanked the two young men and tried vainly to pay for their gas, endow a new clinic, send them to the Shah of Iran, anything to thank them.

The emergency room was cluttered. I felt cozy. A table covered with bloody sheets stood waiting for attention. On another table a long black man, with a towel over his genitals and a crushed leg lying crookedly down from his live body, smiled at me. I sat on a stool while a tiny nurse with enormous black eyes swabbed efficiently at my face. She was alluring, and passionately skillful. A young doctor poked and cut at the dead black leg on the table, and the man laughed softly.

"Does it hurt?" I asked while the nurse got more supplies. "Not on your life," he said in an amused way. "Second time I've done this. My old leg between a stone wall and my motorbike. Then *toubibs* fix me so I don't hurt a-tall."

"Shut up, now," the tiny nurse said, and started to pin my forehead together. "Last time you had a tetanus shot?" I could not remember, so nodded when she shook my shoulder a little and snapped, "Within two years?" She gave me a booster anyway. Two men came in to take me across the hall for X-rays, and as I went out, the Black said laughingly to me, while his *toubib* sliced out a piece of useless old flesh, "Don't worry, Sister!"

There was a lot happening. In my quick trip to the X-ray room, perhaps fifteen feet from the bloody one, I saw two corpses, a child heaving under a sheet on a gurney, several dazed battered people like me. There was no more confusion than there was any effort at all to make the place quiet, attractive, reassuring, as it would be in my country. No potted plants stood in niches, and in the waiting room where my sister sat, there were not enough chairs and children leaned silently against the walls.

I got a quick look at three or four X-rays before they were rushed across the hall to Emergency Surgery: yes, my nose had snapped very neatly; no need to set it; there would be swelling. No concussion.

In Emergency, another young man was clipping the former leg into some semblance of such, and the long Black had snoozed off. The ferocious little nurse was talking with some passion about stitches. "Use plastic clips," the intern said. "Scar," she said, and when he said *clips* again, she came over to me and with a few keen looks into my eyes, onto my face, she dutifully clipped shut the long vertical gash on my forehead. Now and then she felt my wrist. The man with the chopped-up leg was snoring. "Doctor, look here," she said in a peculiar blend of business and sex. He looked, said warmly, "Superb, magnificent!" and went on with his own chore, stitch-snip-stitch. I felt happy that they might sleep together later.

So, on instruction from a tired desk orderly in the huge old hideous hospital, I went the next morning to Dr. Gabil-

laud. I could barely see his door, much less read the information on it, and did not realize until later that it was not his
"office day."

I rang the apartment several times, and heard girls calling,
"Papa! Papa!" Finally he opened the downstairs door, looking fussily scrubbed, in a natty suit and with a dot of shaving
soap in one ear.

"My God," he said. "What has happened to you?"

He put his hand to my shoulder, as he steered me into the
pleasant big room, and when he looked appraisingly at me I
knew, for the first time really, that I was a mess. A three-
inch square of gauze and tape covered most of my forehead,
and another held my nose in place. Both my eyes were
squinty and puffed, with dark bruise marks halfway down
my cheeks: two shiners. My lips were swollen. I smiled carefully at him.

"Well," he said, "at least you have all your teeth! Were
you mugged? Did you fall out of a window?"

So I told him, and increasingly I wondered at the unhesi-
tating kindness of Frenchmen in a dozen cars, out for a
yearly holiday ritual, who stopped or slowed down on the
hectic Corniche to ask if they could help. There I lay on the
pedestrian island, I told Gabby, bloody and dazed, my sister
bending over me, people in cars sounding concerned-generous-
helpful. There we were, on a festive day. And there were
the two young interns, out for some sunshine. . . .

"Of course. Why not?" The doctor sounded testy. I told
him that at home people seemed afraid of becoming involved, scared of lawsuits, of malpractice. "Heathen," he
said. I said that forty citizens could stand watching a woman
be raped and murdered, and not lift a finger to help. "Bar-
baric," he said. "In France we have lived with the law for so
long that we know how and when to make use of it. We are

not afraid of it. In your country you are still so inexperienced, that you are in awe of it. The law is your stern parent, like God, and you fear its punishment. Here we respect it, but only if we respect ourselves more. We use it when we need it."

"But those two young men—they looked thin and poor. They needed a rest. They spent half their free afternoon helping us."

Gabby brushed that away with a surprisingly relaxed gesture of his immaculate hands. "It's their job," he said. "They've already spent years with sick, injured, dying people. In the United States—" and he was off on what became weeks of talk between us, mostly a dialogue about medical problems in our two countries. French students started active patient-care before they opened their first textbooks, he said, and were in the *home* the minute they enrolled in a school. In my country an ambitious intelligent young medical aspirant worked in abstractions, in theories, before he ever delivered a baby or set a bone. By the time an American did his internship he had already decided what branch of medicine he would follow, and by then he might well be wooed by money and power into advanced research. . . .

"We'll never have a Nobel for medicine," Gabby said with some bitterness. "By the time a Frenchman qualifies as a doctor, he has spent a lot of his creative energy on day-and-night care of the sick and is too poor to stop work for further study. Professionally we are a breed of superb-to-piddling country doctors, enslaved by poverty and plain exhaustion."

Gabillaud had two sons and several French protégés in Canada, all medical students. There they would be freer to choose their paths in medicine: they could go from Toronto into the northern wilds of Ontario if some instinctive urge forced them to be frontier bonesetters, and if they wanted the excitements and fat salaries of laboratory research they could head for Detroit, Dallas . . . "In France," he said, "nine out of ten young doctors like the ones you met on Palm Sunday will end up in poor country districts, killing themselves to keep a few ignorant peasants alive."

"But what about those interns and residents at the hospital? They were handsome, skillful, experienced, so young," I said, and he interrupted me. "*Ah,*" he said triumphantly. "They were the pick of the crop! You just happened, my dear friend, to be rescued by two kids doing their last year with Jacques Tatin, one of the finest doctors in Marseille—in France! That was his own pavilion they took you to."

"But it was in a big municipal—"

"*Ah!* Here, aside from having private clinics, very expensive and stylish, many doctors as renowned as my highly respected colleague have their own pavilions in public hospitals, where they train their most promising students from the university school of medicine. The Tatin pavilion is uniquely emergency, to sound out the interns. *All* famous doctors in a town like Marseille, or Paris or Bordeaux, consider it part of their duties to teach on the local faculty. In your case, by neat coincidence, your rescuers happened to be studying under my friend Tatin. He is still fairly young, and brilliant, and he grooms a stable of the most promising colts in French medicine, including his own son. Of course he has his private clinic—no need for Junior to head for Toronto! Tatin is a magnificent kidney man—"

"But my nose," I said. "And the young doctor working on that leg! Urology?"

"Precisely!" Gabby said. "Men who can intern with Tatin have already spent several years, perhaps their best ones, working in every branch of the art of medicine. Half of them

will never go much further than their own practices in provincial towns. A special few will end by being rich, covered
with decorations, safe with their own famous patients in their
own elegant clinics. A few will be like me, or rather the way
I *was*, head surgeons in big hospitals and still with their own
practices. I'm now a gynecologist, you know from my little
sign. But I can recognize an allergic bronchial cough when
I hear it. And I am very good at stitchery, thanks to two years
in an emergency pavilion in Bordeaux, much like Tatin's.
And I wish that young rascal had not put clips on your
forehead. I could have made that scar as unimportant as a
wrinkle. Now it's a scowl. But of course I'd have to charge
you."

By then this was a quiet joke with us, well along in our
dialogue. His first fee, the night he came to the apartment,
had so plainly startled me that from then on he somewhat
sardonically translated every sum for me, in "old francs"
and then "de Gaulle." The day he stared from across his
desk at my poor crumpled face, he waived any fee. The
others were all unpredictable: about two dollars when he
wrote prescriptions, a dollar now and then, once about eight
when I had to undress and go into the converted kitchen for
probings. (This was when housewives of low means did not
blink at paying five or six dollars a pound for the Sunday
roast.) I suppose that in almost five months, while I grate-
fully renewed some contact with the French language, I
spent about thirty dollars.

Prescriptions were costlier. The corner pharmacist continued his first disapproval of me, when I firmly paid cold cash
for his magic elixirs, potions, pastilles. I tried to explain to
him that I did not feel entitled to French Medicare, since I
was a transient foreigner and paid almost no taxes. "It's
there, Madame," he said reprovingly. "Take it. Make the

most of a good thing," and every time that I did not, he shrugged as if with fatalistic disapproval of my stupidity. And to my continuing astonishment there seemed to be almost none of the maze of paperwork (*paperasserie,* which sounds funnier in English than in French) that is accepted as a necessary and routine evil at home—and of course in some branches of French officialdom like the postal service.

When I went to Emergency at the big public hospital in Marseille, the desk orderly asked for my name and address as I left. The sexy wee surgical nurse had already told me to return at once if I felt feverish, and in ten days if not, and had dismissed me fiercely as another bloody body was rolled into her room. When I went back, the second Wednesday after Palm Sunday, she spotted me at once in the hall and said angrily, "Oh, *you!* This is not your day! Oh, yes—it is!" She stood on tiptoe to rip the old tired bandage off my head, nodded with a dazzling smile, and pushed me into her room, which was gorier than before, but empty.

I sat again on the low stool, and she swabbed at me as fast as a bird pecking for grain. It hurt a little, but I knew that she was in no way careless or ignorant. She stood back to take a long satisfied look. "Superb! Magnificent," she murmured, since the handsome intern was not there to say it. "Now *out!* Don't come back!" And I was in the hall before I could even try to thank her. I thought, she is like a delicious Provençal olive, firm, small, succulent, with a forthright bite to her flavor. . . .

The desk orderly asked, "Dismissed? Name, address?" He gave me an indecipherable written description of my outpatient care noted by l'Assistance Publique de Marseille, number CICH 1428, and asked me to sign it, so that my social insurance could pay the bill. He looked with frank astonishment at me when I explained that since I was a temporary resident, and a foreigner, I myself wanted to pay. Finally he said, "You mean you are a *tourist?*" He shrugged as if I were therefore mad. "The bill [you poor benighted nitwit, his voice added without words], Madame, is forty-four hundred ninety francs!" Thanks to Dr. Gabillaud, and a few fish-women on the Quai des Belges who liked to startle visitors with the "Old and New," I did not even blink, and handed out forty-four francs and ninety centimes, and he signed my receipt and bowed sadly at me from his chair.

I had thus rashly paid about nine dollars for two visits to Emergency, a booster shot against tetanus, a lot of bandage and tape, and several X-rays and six clips. When I told Gabby all this, he smiled and said casually, "You are obviously either idealistic or merely stubborn. But here in the office, my poor lady, you must pay and pay! I milk the rich tourists, to treat for nothing a handful of penniless *pieds noirs* from Algeria. . . ."

And not long ago, on the radio in California, I heard a newscast by a bedazzled young reporter who told of having broken his leg in Marseille. He was hospitalized for two nights, in a cast, and then allowed to hop around until the bone was correctly healed, with several visits to the municipal clinic where it had been set. Finally he was discharged, and apologetically required to pay an extra sum of almost four dollars for a special metal brace the doctors had put into the plaster with his permission, so that he could go back to his work sooner. That was all, he reported dreamily, and I smiled with complicity and thought of all the American doctors who must be tut-tutting his subversive socialistic message. . . .

This report of mine could be a chatty incident about the avaricious cold scheming cheating lying Frenchman so often described by us tourists, but it is really about what happened

to me on Palm Sunday, 1973, on the Corniche Kennedy. Or
perhaps is it more truly about how I managed subconsciously
to prolong my official visits to a doctor who spoke beautiful
gabby French?

By the time my sister and I had to leave Marseille, she was
philosophical about my lengthy visits to Gabillaud, and by
now she feels as I do, that we've all met before, in Simenon's
stories about Commissioner Maigret. Maigret's best friend
has always been Dr. Pardon. The Maigrets and the Pardons
dine together once a week or so, and know exactly what favorite dishes to serve each other, and when the two men can find
an evening free from murders and childbirths, they talk
and talk . . . about puzzling cases, even about themselves.
And we listen, delighted Peeping Toms. . . .

Yes, Gabby is another Pardon, a true "neighborhood doctor," after all his less constricted years. He is concerned about
his patients, and deliberately involved in what is happening
to them, what will happen next, why, where. I would like
to see him again, but there is no excuse to. I still scowl, and always shall. But I still have all my teeth, and could smile at
him. And then we could slide into a delicious little Gabby-fest
about the authenticity of Rodin's head of Cézanne on the
fountain in Aix, or about the increasing ambiguity of the
AMA toward socialized medicine, or or or. . . .

Chapter 6

THE
GAMBLERS

I

Sometimes I wonder if I sound a little tetched about cab-drivers in Marseille . . . if I choose them on purpose, if I have some compulsion about savoring their unpredictably raffish behavior.

The truth is that while I lived there with my sister Norah in 1973 and later, I spoke with few people except waiters, shopkeepers, and cabbies and myself. Norah was thoroughly involved in research and was gone all or much of most days, while her accent improved in the company of elderly librarians, eccentric scholars, and fellow-delvers. I, on the other hand, spoke an increasingly creaky and careless French, still better than that of many of the people I used it with but not challenging, so that by the time we were packing to return to California, and my professor from the University of Dijon (1929–31!) came to bid us a quick return, he held his hands over his ears in disgust.

I said, "I can't help it. I've met perhaps two educated Frenchmen in five months. I talk . . . communicate . . . simplistically with people who are as alien here as I am: waiters from Iran or Egypt, cabbies from Sicily and Algiers and God knows where. . . ." But when I told him a little of what they talked about, he shrugged forgivingly and said, "You'll be all right."

Of course it is one thing to sit in a café and read *Le Meridional* and *Le Monde* and sip a vermouth-gin until Nórah shows up after a morning at the City Library in the Bourse, and another to entrust one's life to a taxi driver. The latter experience has, perforce, more intensity; it is more memorable, whether or not it should be. In a café, one can get up and walk away. In a cab, the set of the driver's shoulders, his smell, the frightening instant of meeting his eyes in the rear-view mirror (what kind, bloodshot or jaundiced or drug-dazed color): all that is a vital challenge, and often as pungent as ether.

Norah may meet me at our apartment with the jaunty news that while Artemis, the Greek goddess who protected Protis in his surprising nuptials in Massilia in 600 B.C., had eighteen breasts, the Christian saint Mary Magdalen in perhaps A.D. 60 had only two . . . BUT . . . they are said by the local devout near her shrine today to have flowed with copious (and of course holy) milk when she was a very old saint indeed. That's fine, that's great, I say to the avid scholar. Then I tell her about my latest cabdriver.

Today, for instance, there were no taxis in the stand at the Place de Gaulle, opposite the Bourse, but I did not feel like walking home and knew I need only wait. It was not raining. One came sliding into its place up the curb toward the Opera, and I noticed without really noticing that a young couple with some bags or suitcases stopped it and that it then came down toward me, where passengers were supposed to wait. I got in, and told the driver my address. He was a heavyset man of perhaps sixty, with longish grey-white hair and the broad rubbery face of a former clown or vaudevillian.

As we started, the young woman ran up to the taxi and rapped on the window and asked why he had passed her by, and he said loud and firm, "Because you stink," and drove off.

I decided that I was once more in the weapon of a maniac, helpless bullet in gun, so I sat back and asked mildly, "Why did you say that?" He could either answer me in the same manner, in a reasonable way, or he could explode, and since I was trapped anyway, it did not much matter to me. He chose the first path, and said, "Because she does."

"How do you know, with the window closed?"

"I know by her face," he said flatly. "She's a Gypsy, and Gypsies stink."

I started to say, always in the mild and nonreproachful way, "But after all she is a—" and he interrupted me. "Don't tell me, lady, that she's a human being, which I knew you were going to say, because Gypsies are not human. They do not qualify. And they have a terrible smell, because they are damned."

I asked what the smell was like, and he said, always in a matter-of-fact way, not as if he were humoring me or playing a rehearsed scene, "It is purely and simply *le suint. Le suint gitan.*" (I thought I knew that it was something about old sour sweat on dirty bodies, but I looked it up when I got back to the apartment and it meant a kind of greasy ooze.) I said something like "Oh," and he manipulated a couple of neat cornerings.

He was a relaxed sure driver, which is the only way to be in Marseille and probably everywhere. Then he said in an almost fatherly way, "I doubt that you have ever lived with them." I said that I had known a few and observed them whenever I could, and he said, "Yes, but you've never lived with them, *lived*. I have. And they stink."

This seemed the natural end to the conversation on that subject, and in a few blocks we went on to how many pleasure boats as opposed to fishing boats there were in the Old Port. He told a lot I had been spending several days trying to dig out of officials for my own satisfaction, and the rest of the ride was informative and pleasant, and I was glad that I had grown up enough not to be upset by varied prejudices, at least to the point of jumping out of a cab, which I did once on Union Square in San Francisco.

That time I knew that I could not listen to one more word from the driver, who was a proud Midwestern member of the John Birch Society and currently loudmouthed about the subversive hippies floating amiably over the lawns and into the bushes of the public park. He was intolerable. But the chauffeur in Marseille was quiet, reasonable, and absolutely fixed in his loathing of the Gypsy smell, and I felt interested in both his deliberate hatred of a whole race because of perhaps a few examples (or even one), and his dispassionate candor. He used words well, without affectation, and there was no feeling at all that he was trying to make me know that he was not a taxi driver for want of anything better, which often happens with the talkative ones, nor that he was trying to teach me something . . . set me right.

I was glad that I had not sounded outraged or preachy to him, in my first resignation about being caught once more in a rapidly moving vehicle with a madman at the controls. He had his own dignity, which included the belief, for no matter what private reasons, that Gypsies have a special ghastly smell, which proves that they are damned and not quite human, or perhaps that they are not human at all and therefore *must* smell that way. What business was it of mine? I had asked him as a professional driver to take me home, not to explain his raison d'être, and he managed to do both in an expert and unaggressive way.

I remain basically affronted by what he said so firmly, because it is against my hopeful human yearnings, but since he did not affront anything else, I listened that day and perhaps even learned something, if not about Gypsies or him, about myself.

At least he did not make direct or sly chitchat about "Arabs," the current hate-objects in Marseille. I would have turned mute, not trusting myself, and he might have driven with petulance or ferocity, neither of which is enjoyable to the captive passenger.

This interchange did nothing, of course, for my accent, and not much more for my sister's interest in my currently peculiar life style, and/but I am probably relieved that it went off amiably. We all survived, in most ways.

I I

This is not so much about a young man in Marseille in 1973 as it is about people of any age, anywhere, I suppose. He was perhaps twenty-five, short, with the beautiful silver-copper skin of some Algerians, and soft black hair down to his shoulders, in studied waves and strands. He was a taxi driver.

I had to wait for several minutes at the official taxi stand on the Place de Gaulle, because it was shortly before noon and raining hard, after a few springlike but faintly ominous hours of darkening skies. This kind of weather will drive

to shelter the natives of Marseille almost as firmly as do
the occasional gusty winds, which whether they come from
the Swiss Alps or Italy or across from Spain, or even
correctly down the Rhône Valley, are generally called "le
mistral." This word is always said with a fatalistic shrug,
part affection and part resignation, as if to condone and
accept human patience in the face of natural forces, and
indeed it has long been held that if a *crime passionel* can be
proved to have been committed while the mistral blew, the
criminal is exonerated. Such is not the case with the *other*
wind, the tramontane, which according to several sources
blows from anywhere except down the Rhône but actually is
a cold northeast wind from near the Italian border. Some
natives say the weather is deliciously clear and sparkling while
it blows, and to others it is vicious enough to fill the air with
flying roof tiles. One fisherman told me that the only trouble
he ever had was when the mistral and the tramontane were
blowing at the same time. "Then the boat dances a little,"
he said. Other fishermen have told me that the two winds
can never happen at the same time. How would I know? All
I know about the day I met the young man is that I myself
would say that there was no real mistral, no real tramontane,
but only a good March rainstorm. . . .

As I worked my way down the line of people waiting for
taxis, one harassed-looking lawyer or broker invited me under
his umbrella, and I was so taken aback by his storm-bound
casualness, knowing he would never do such a thing without
formal introductions in fairer weather, that I spoke unusually
bad French, which took him aback too, if only temporarily.
When his cab rolled up he hopped in without another word
and I was left in the downpour, resolving never to speak such
vile stuttering syllables again, even to myself.

My cab came next, and I dove into it and said good

morning. Usually taxi drivers respond, if they have not said it first and often with embellishments, but I looked with some slight speculation at the young silky-haired hack, and said in the most impeccable enunciation I could call up from the courses in diction I took at the University of Dijon in 1929 and on, something like "Please take me to 41 avenue de la Corse." I did it well, as if to prove that my linguistic blur under the stranger's umbrella had been a passing aberration.

The young man said "O.K.," and then buried his head between the palms of his well-shaped hands, and I could hear the rain on the roof of the car. I knew that there was pressure on the cabbies because of the rain, and that it was almost noon rush hour, and also that sometimes people have to withdraw from the world and start over again. I have a fairly clear empathy with taxi drivers, and I felt that I should let this beautiful young man gather his forces after God knows what ordeal, professional or otherwise.

The chauffeurs in line behind him were sounding their horns, and finally his hands dropped to the wheel, and he sighed deeply, perhaps with resignation. I said, always with a clear and well-planned pattern of the requisite phrases, fully believing that he, like several other drivers since the west end of La Corderie has been renamed La Corse, would wonder where in Hell my address was, "Generally, if one so wishes, one can reach my address by taking either the Rue Sainte or going out on the Rive Neuve."

He shot off, but at the first traffic wait he said fiercely, never turning around, that drivers don't need directions and that they know where they are going and a few other such statements. I had heard them before, from amateurs anyway, and never as ferociously, and I agreed with him (the docile captive, the trapped rat . . .).

He drove skillfully, coldly. When we got near my place,

which is on the opposite side of the street from his direction, I said something like, "The number I gave you is on the left side, but I'll get out across from it, here . . ." and he slammed to a halt. I started to open the door, and he said, "Just a minute!" and I thought again of people who feel angry for reasons other people don't know, and of all the puzzlement of trying to function and even exist in this climate, this climate of puzzlement. I closed the door again, to listen to him.

He continued, with his eyes straight forward, "We drivers are all licensed, in Marseille. We don't accept directions from passengers. In order to get a license we must learn every street in the city and the environs. We know how to get anywhere at any time, and we do not need the advice of casual pickups . . . of officious passengers who think they can tell us where to go and how to get there, in their school-teacher prissy foreign accents."

He stayed low-voiced but explosive. "I'll explain to you," he said with a mad patience, "that it costs every one of us plenty to get a license, because we have to know the right people and keep them happy. So certainly, with my legal hard-won papers, I do not need your free instructions. My qualifications are as good as anybody's, and I refuse to submit to being told like a schoolboy, as for instance right this minute, to go out to the Corniche in order to turn around to a third-rate hotel door."

I not only had never mentioned going out to the Corniche but it had not occurred to me to, as he whirled in a U-turn to stop in front of the door. What is more, I had not told him I was going to a hotel at all. But I looked at the back of his furious young head, covered with carefully arranged lock-lets, and I thought a little about being in a huge high-powered sprawl like Marseille, within a so-called minority circle, and the tough routine of getting a license through every possible pipeline that fed through that circle, and then of having personal gnawings and woes. And I simply paid him with the usual tip and got out, into a wide rushing gutter and a heavy rain.

I thanked him impersonally, and he did not respond, which is unusual in Marseille, and I felt that he was far off again, and might well have to bury his face in his hands. I did not look back, in case this was so.

I I I

Like many people who find themselves spectator sports in most of the current games, I consider taxi drivers a good gamble, and I bet on them every time.

I manage to let most of them feel that I not only trust them with life and limb, but that I think they must be interesting and have something to tell me, something nobody else could. This maneuver brings out the best, nine times in ten, and is conducive to excellent driving through the dirtiest parts of New York, down the worst hills in San Francisco, around the most horrendous carrefours in Paris and Marseille. And in return for the attention the drivers pay to road and me, in that order, I am genuinely grateful for their personal as well as professional reactions to my guile, and I think they enjoy this too.

Mostly.

Once in New York and once in Paris I knew I was captive of a dangerously insane driver, and was ready in a few seconds of acceptance for either hospital or merciful death. Often, too, I have been conscious of overfatigue or personal stress in the man in front of me. Mostly, though, I have been

able with not too much effort to settle into a relaxed con-
finement with a normally mad cabbie, and assume that he will
indeed take me to X Street and the corner of Z, and tell me
a few titbits on the way.

Sometimes taxi drivers are new to their cabs, or to the
hiring company or even the town. But once I got one who was
simply *new*. The only recognizable and reassuring thing
about him was the cloud of *pastis* that moved into the cab
with him: I knew that I was still in Marseille, even if he
did not.

He looked as if he had lived well. He was finely tailored,
in an almost stockbroker style, barely balding, a trim man
just touching successful middle age. He came out of a little
bar across from the taxi stand on the Place de Gaulle,
where I had been waiting by a row of blandly empty cabs.
I was ready to stamp away, frustrated by the plain fact
that drivers have to relieve themselves now and then, and
even drink and eat and gossip a little. I was surprised to see
this man walk straight toward me and the front cab and
then get in it, for certainly he was not a real part of the bar,
of the Place, of the cab itself.

He smiled a little at me, and with my intrinsic willingness
to gamble one more time I got in too, and gave him the
address I hoped to reach. He smiled more, and suddenly I
realized that he was scared almost silly. I wondered if he
was stealing the cab. He fumbled with key, ignition, all that,
and plainly had never been at such a wheel before. His
shoulders in their handsome suit looked vaguely defeated.

"Do you know where to go?" I asked bluntly, as if to slap
him awake, and it was the beginning of a lengthy dialogue,
while we moved uncertainly from lane to lane through two
of the worst intersections in Marseille, and went east on two
westbound-only streets, and in general learned a lot. He did,

anyway, for it was indeed the first time he had ever driven a taxi, as well as the first time he ever saw the city. We both saw more than believable, because of the traffic lanes. What can you do if only the left lane turns up by St. Victor and you are in the right one, except head helplessly through the tunnel, on and on, and then try to double back . . . ?

He could see or feel that I was almost catatonically unrattled, and I saw and felt at once that he knew how to drive, as such, so we simply cruised through a large part of the Rive Neuve area while he told me in upper-class Parisian that he had dropped into the cabbies' bar on the Place and accepted a bet one of the men had made, after several rounds offered by the big-city toff, to handle his hack for one fare. The man said that he was looking for local color, and we both laughed comfortably about the notorious sense of humor of the Marseillais as he wobbled into another wrong turn.

He was sweating a little, but was collected. I felt at ease, in my familiar taxi-mood of fatalism. We finally got to my door, and I gave him the usual tip in spite of his tailoring, and he bowed, thanked me, and said, "Never again, Madame." I hoped he would find his way back to the café, but did not say so.

One thing he had said was that he could never have done such a crazy thing if he had been cold sober, but this did not bother me. Sobriety is a rare and dubious virtue, if that at all, with people under heavy stress like cabbies, cooks, and even politicians. It is often an improvement, for them and for us, to be able to disregard every bothersome detail of survival except the immediacy of the business, and to stay clear in the center of a blur. This nirvana is of course unattainable to most thirsty people, and its pursuit is hard on the human liver as well as human lives. Occasionally, though, alcohol is a godsend, and I feel that several *pastis* drunk in an unfamiliar town got one driver and me through a potentially dreadful dare.

My sister and I discussed this highly debatable theory, as well as my miraculous arrival at the right address, and hoped that the lost Parisian was safely home again, a wiser man. We began making little jokes about him in comparison with other drivers we had met during the months in Marseille. Most of the time there, we walked, but in heavy rains or moments of unexpected weariness we headed for two or three stands we had spotted, and revived ourselves with the heady excitement of the real gambler before Chance itself. And it added an extra zip, to know that at least we would not be the temporary captives of my own gambling driver. "Let's blow ourselves to a taxi," we'd say after a morning in the Flower Market. "Our favorite tourist is gone, so we'll make it home. . . ."

About two months after my boozy encounter, we had to go through some hours of unexpected hassling with the French Railway System, to send several cartons of stuff-junk-rubble back to California. And right there in the office we had to rewrap everything, retie it, retape it, and then rewrite three labels and three other papers for each carton, and although the two young men who took care of us were nicer than anyone could be in this whole wide world, and were polite and jolly and in all ways superbly compassionate and gentle, my sister and I found ourselves thoroughly shaken when we finally got out of the local branch of the Société Nationale des Chemins de Fer.

I said flatly that I did not know if I could walk to the nearest café chair: I was trembly in my marrow . . . and why, when the young men had been so nice? My sister said that she felt very odd too. We decided, as we headed for the Quai des Belges and the dimmest quietest corner of a bar that had one, that we were organically, psychosomatically, hopelessly at war with bureaucracy itself. Furthermore, we were fighting repressed pique or anger or plain disgust because all our first laborious wrappings and labelings had been torn off before our eyes. By the time we had either revived or else numbed our nerves with a drink, and got this settled, we felt better, and strong enough to walk toward the Place de Gaulle and its taxi stand. We could even joke a little, and say that today of all days it was lucky that we did not have to cope with my pal from Paris.

Of course it was he who came out of the little café as we waited by the head cab. We both knew him without a word between us. He was as trimly tailored as before, but needed a shave. He wore the familiar cloud of *pastis*, like an invisible toga. He did not look at us as he slid into his seat.

I gave him the same address, and he glanced at me in his rear-view mirror, but I knew then as I know now that he did not remember either my accent or what it had once said.

He was at home, this time, with the key, the switch, the wheel. But he got out a map and looked quickly at it, before he started a smooth expert drive to our place. None of us said anything, for various reasons. Once there, he manipulated a fancy U-turn on the wide busy street, and leaned over to open the door for us. He smiled a little, thanked us for his tip, and then burst out, "I've been here exactly two months, and tomorrow I take my taxi-license tests!" He sounded jaunty and excited. We congratulated him, and he drove neatly away, and we felt Full Circle as we went silently to our apartment.

Chapter 7

THE FOOD OF
ARTEMIS

It has been said, and rightly, that a tomato of Provence tastes different from that grown from the same seed in another soil and air. It will have a pungency, an earthy savor, and a smell that are robust but not coarse. It makes understandable at once, without words, why the men of the South of France know that the reason their women ("strong, wild, fertile," they have been called) are more lastingly seductive than others is that they are fed from the cradle on the local love apples.

These fruits, sliced fresh from the gardens, cooked into every conceivable dish, made into thick pastes for winter sustenance; alone or with a little olive oil; stewed-baked-grilled in countless ways: tomatoes in Marseille stand alone or blend happily with eggs, fish, meats. They are true kitchen stalwarts, like the human females who feed on them.

This same salty vitality is everywhere else in Provence, as far as I can see. Women, tomatoes, children and men, herbs and trees . . . and sheep and the small black fighting bulls: they all have it. The rice of the Camarque, for instance: it was almost unknown until after the fall of Dien Bien Phu, when France's Oriental supplies were cut off and the desperate government drained miles of salt marshes in the Rhône delta and made paddies. These produced, almost violently, one of the most unusual and delicious grains I ever tasted, hard and strongly salted. It soon became sought out, first to surprise people used to the comparatively delicate rices of Indo-China, and then to satisfy a real craving for its noisy personality. It was a match for the Provençal tomato, and indeed it was a perfect foil for the whole cuisine of the area.

Suddenly, and while the fame of Camarquais rice was spreading fast, politics and an international thirst for light modest wines helped the government rip out most of the flourishing paddies, drain them, and prepare the salty old silt of the delta for miles and miles of vineyards. Quick-growing, undistinguished grape stock was planted with a speed that made serious vintners of the "North" (really any of them, North, East, or West of the "Côtes du Rhône" and Lyon) shake their heads in somewhat sardonic disbelief.

The first crops were pressed and blended and bottled with shocking speed, and then bought with unheard-of local enthusiasm in small shops, huge supermarkets. The wines, light and mostly as undistinguished as their roots, were adequate for drinking, easy on the palate and the pocketbook, and pleasant everyday companions to Provençal food. They were candid in their origins, and they continue to sell phenomenally well in their own region, produced as they are by both the large cooperatives and the smaller growers, for quick consumption. And they have a dryness that makes them truly "sand wines," sprung up almost as fast as the rice before them, and the marsh grasses before the rice, on the edge of the Mediterranean.

All this durable strength, this mysterious saltiness, is what gives the food as well as the wine of Marseille a zest that I have never known anywhere else.

Of course there can be dreadful dishes there, just as there can be infamous bottles. Every kitchen and winery has its own share of idiots, rascals, and wretches. But in general, and over a period of more than forty years, I honestly think I have had an almost untarnished succession of exciting, amusing meals in Marseille. As a stranger, I have never eaten in a private home there, although once I was invited to an alfresco luncheon in the country near the Mont Ste.-Victoire, by some Marseillais I wish I still knew. It was one of the most delicious meals I ever ate, and the conversation was so light and witty that I can still smile about it.

As an almost professional ghost, however, I have developed a fairly dependable nose for good public eating places, from the most stylish-but-honest to the lowliest-but-honorable. I know that nearly all French towns can boast of one kind or the other, and that the big cities are filled with them, but for me Marseille remains the chosen magical mysterious One. And I think it is because of the peculiar liveliness of what grows behind it on the ancient soil, and especially what swims and creeps and slithers at its watery gates. There is no doubt about it: freshly caught fish, scaly or in the shell, have a different flavor and texture and *smell* there than in any other port in the world. The flavor is intense and assertive, no matter how delicate: a *loup*, for instance, will remain its own self even when it is grilled over dry fennel leaves and then flamed with an extra douse of Pernod. Texture is fine or coarse or succulent or crisp, depending on whether one eats a fresh sardine, a fillet of tuna, a raw mussel. And the smell is so pure that it is as heady as the first breath from a dark winery cellar just hosed down—or from a silent printing-pressroom if one reacts as I do to good ink and paper.

Any reputable open-front fish shop in Provence will smell this way, but the best place there, and perhaps in the whole world, is the old Criée on the Rive Neuve in Marseille. This great airy vaulted room is the public wholesale auction place for the area, and opens after midnight, and is closed again by five in the morning, except for swabbers in hip boots washing every spot, every trestle and board and crate and ladder, with stiff brushes and fierce jets of water from their long hoses. In another hour or so the place is locked, silent, but while the night's bidding went on, it was one of the noisiest places ever dreamed of, somewhat like the "capital pit" of a great stock exchange but with an utterly different vibration to its screaming roar. This is perhaps because there are always many women there, with the harsh strident voices of classical fishwives, often gruff and bellowing but always female.

And at La Criée, at its wildest peak of trading and out-bidding, with dealers and fishmongers and agents shoving and shouting around the trestle tables heaped with the finest of the available catch, there is never any smell of sweat, or garlic, or anything but exquisitely fresh clean briny *fish*.

Outside along the Rive Neuve the real activity starts a few hours before La Criée opens, with countless huge refrigerated trucks rolling in from Normandy, Brittany, the Gironde. Their lobsters and Channel soles and herrings, their several kinds of oysters, are packed in special white styrofoam boxes, tightly closed, but even so, a mist of pure *fish* manages to escape from them as they are rushed into other trucks and headed for Lyon or Switzerland or ships in the Port, or are trundled into the cool dim vault of La Criée to be ready for its violent predawn awakening.

It is foolhardy to try to pick one's way at night along that part of the Rive Neuve, landside, when the trucks are coming and going. Men unload the white crates with deft speed, and see only what they must do. But when Norah and I lived above the end of the Quai, we often walked home from "town" at the most hectic moments, and never once tripped or got bumped into, or even cursed at. We could have been two moths.

Probably we would have been kicked away, if we'd been cats. (It is odd to realize that I have never seen a cat near the Criée, nor the morning fish boats along the Quai des Belges at the end of the Port, nor the many fish restaurants all around. Is the smell too fresh and saline for them? Is there too much cold water in the harbor, on the floors, sloshing everywhere? Have centuries of being unwelcome given Marseille's cat-world an inborn sense of what places to avoid? Or do cats really like fish as much as they are supposed to?)

Most of the nearby restaurants, from fine to humble, display their daily fish in front of or near their doors, so that clients must pass them and be lured by the gleam and glow of color, the fragile smell. On the hotter days a coolness hovers over the ice-packed slanted counters, and iodine and salt waver up almost tangibly from the beds of seaweeds the fish lie on. Often, in a window opening onto the street, as crown of the display inside, there will be a kind of *pièce montée*, a Dali or Carême sculpture of one stunningly graceful *loup*, posed for an endless second with a great pink shrimp in its mouth, as it leaps from a high wave of smaller red and blue and silver fishes over the piles of oysters, mussels, urchins, clams. . . .

Once I saw such a fantasy in an elegant restaurant window on the Quai des Belges: a ring of small lobsters dancing on their tails, holding claws in a circle around a great humped black fish with glaring eyes. On his back were two big lobsters, side-saddle, holding his reins in their own claws. The pavement was of hundreds of fresh sardines laid in patterns bordered with purple sea urchins, and a hidden electric fan made all the lobsters' delicate feelers wave in rhythm. The whole thing was a past/present dream, subtly nightmarish but hilarious. It was extravagant, and meant to last a few hours at best, and I still see it, and smell its airy salt.

I do not remember anything at all about eating fish the first time I was in Marseille in 1929, although the strong-voiced women selling their husbands' catch from the stern of each little boat backed up to the Quai des Belges seemed to have chosen an enviably sane job to me, a refugee from the dank academic walls of Dijon. (By now the catch is unloaded in a flash onto little trestle tables set up on the Quai, and usually the wives are there to sell, while the boats head out to sea again, or dawdle until the tables can be folded and stored on deck for the next day. As one hefty old woman said to me in about 1970, "For the first time in my life, I don't have a stiff neck, from yelling up at all you nitwits on the Quai—")

The next time I went to the Old Port I felt infinitely removed from the shy tongue-bound bride of some three years before. Dijon was behind. I knew what I was hearing and saying, and how to eat and drink better than thus far in my life. For our last meal in the country we loved so surely, my husband and younger sister Norah and I went to the Mont Ventoux. I have since watched it grow elegant and then decline, but on that bright May Day in 1932 or so, it was simple and very welcoming to us, and to celebrate (not leaving, but the return, any time, no matter how or how

soon!), we ate a majestic bouillabaisse, and drank amply of
a bone-dry white wine from the bone-dry white country a
little farther down the coast. Perhaps the fish stew was especially good, as it can be. Perhaps it was "one more
bouillabaisse," as is generally the case. Certainly it did not
make me a passionate devotee of the local attraction, and I
think that since that far day I may have eaten it only four or
five times. But then it was a perfect dish to help us say
Until Soon Again. It was rich and fumy, of course, with
warmth for the belly and sustenance for the spirit, and we
were ready for whatever might be ahead when M. Sicard
pushed us gently into a taxi, after one last glass of the family
marc with him. "Drive fast," he called after us. "Until
soon," we called back.

But it was a few years and several new lives before the
next meal in that upstairs dining room. M. Sicard had retired
to his vineyards. The restaurant had lost its stairway down
to the Quai, and was hushed and elegant, with an entrance
onto the Canebière, and a delicately fragrant oyster stand in
the downstairs hall, all lemons and wet seaweed and breathing shellfish. I was with somewhat hushed elegant people
too. We stopped and chose the oysters we would eat, and
went on up to the new room, glass on two sides, with the
whole Port below us. It was lovely, and as different from
the old place as I was different from the young student-wife.

That restaurant was excellent, and stayed so for perhaps
thirty more years, a record in such a chancy game. Affluent
important locals liked it, and shared it with their foreign
friends and victims, and well-heeled worldly travellers knew
about it, and I saw some of the most beautifully dressed
women of my life there. The first time I ate by one of its
twinkling window-walls, I embarrassed my severely correct
hostess by ordering a dozen Belons for the first course, and

another dozen for the second. They were as perfect as they had smelled, on the way past them up the stairs, and I like to think that my discreet but obvious enjoyment softened the social shocks that continued to fall on my proud old lady.

For a long time I returned almost compulsively to that upstairs room on the Quai des Belges, always for lunch and always with great satisfaction of many senses: the glitter or sullen storminess of the Vieux Port; the good waiters and the maître d'hôtel and the cloakroom matron, most of them greeting me as if I had been there the past week and not several years before; the smell of the waiting shellfish going up the stairs with us.

But in 1971 the oyster stand was gone. I felt apprehensive. The headwaiter told me that the "new clientele" ignored it, so that the shell-opener had nothing to do downstairs that a kitchen apprentice could not do less expensively upstairs. He shrugged. He looked dismal, with well-trained remoteness.

In about 1973, I think, I got a whiff of real disillusion, when the staircase and even the tables wore advertisements of somebody like JoJo and his Magical Electric Organ, playing every night during dinner, any tune from any country. Goodbye, part of me said painfully.

Three years later I went back to the old corner. There was a high wooden wall around it, so that the entrance was blocked off. At night there were dim lights upstairs, but no signs of waiters or diners, and in the quick-order-café-brasserie on the street level were notices pointing to an inside stairway to "Our Deluxe Dining Room." I ate in the brasserie once, because it was a night for soup and a salad after some high days of downing shellfish in every logical guise as well as straight from the shell . . . and nobody ever went upstairs. I shrugged. I felt disconsolate, or much worse, and although fairly well trained, I was unable to be remote about my innate sense of loss. Something had gone, and it was too late to do anything but realize how good it had been, while it had seemed a natural part of my life, something always to head back to.

Now, when I return to Marseille, how can that restaurant *not* be there? I have been betrayed, and I know this must happen again and more than once before I too stop.

The Two Sisters, for instance: they cannot possibly live forever on the Rive Neuve! Every time I see them, and all the indefatigable nieces, lovers, husbands, cousins, who work in their small fishhouse, they look younger, or at least in good fettle. They serve at a mad dauntless speed, and with such apparent enthusiasm and delight that it is tonic to be near them.

There are, of course, a lot of other such restaurants along that quay, and some of them are, or can be, very good. One or two are always bad enough to fail, day after tomorrow, or are rebuilding from past errors. A lot of their clients are Marseillais, supersensitive to fish and its perfections, but they are also tourist lures, complete with tough teasing women who stand in the doorways and almost blackmail the passersby to come in—eat the best bouillabaisse ever made. . . .

This technique, as I well know, is painful to many blond blue-eyed visitors. The *entraîneuse* is out there raucously taunting people on the sidewalks, who amble along looking with mild curiosity for a good meal, and it is an embarrassing circus to the tender-skinned Northerners who accidentally find themselves on the Rive Neuve. If they are extravagant or cowed enough to order lobster, the harridan will stand on the sidewalk right by their table, and point through the window at everything on their plates, loudly drawing a small crowd to gape and envy and perhaps push on into the restaurant. Italians and even Germans can take this noisy exposure in stride, but the English turn as red as their fine fare, and wish they were anywhere but in Marsales, "that most sordid and filthy hole," as one of their compatriots called it in about 1800.

I think that I have eaten once or even many times in every fishhouse on that side of the Vieux Port, over the last forty-odd years. They change, of course, and occasionally die, or linger pitifully past their prime, half-empty. For several years now, a small Chinese restaurant has survived where a good fish place used to be. It smells all right, but of soy sauce and mushrooms rather than, more properly, of seaweed and shimmering cold fishes and plump shells. One or two of the places are stylishly decorated: modern "rustic" furniture, copper pans and Camarquais cattle-prods on the walls, flowers towering over the whimsical displays of fish or strawberry tarts. There are a few plainer places with paper tablecloths and napkins, ample servings of fish soup, unlabeled rosé in liter bottles. Every class of restaurant is crowded, all year round, as long as its fish is of today's catch and is treated with respect.

The Two Sisters' place is in between, aesthetically at least. It has a small glassed terrace with five or six tables pinched into it, a little restaurant, an upstairs room for celebrations along with a window display of fish and a few proud lobsters languidly waving their feelers, and a steeply banked stand of shellfish with an elderly relative opening them with feverish skill as customers order trays of whatever they want and can afford. The trays are put on the tables on wire legs about ten inches high, and the diners pick what is nearest to them if they are polite . . . or reach for what looks plumpest on the far side. People in the money, though, trying to impress a girl-friend or the boss, or ignorant of the current value of the franc in dollars, pounds, lire, marks, will usually eat oysters:

expensive, so fresh that the delicate dark flanges recoil a little at the touch. They are for special treats.

One good way to taste two or three of them, not the costliest Belons of course, but tangy lesser breeds, is to order a *panaché*, a mixed platter of every shellfish on hand. It is pretty, and fun. Like all other such platters, the open shells lie on a bed of cold seaweed, sometimes laid over cracked ice in warm weather, with halved lemons in the center. There will be one or two kinds of mussels: small darkish ones cultivated at Bouziques, very pungent; large fat ones with pale or orange-colored flesh, from the rocks along the coast. There will be a few urchins, and at the Two Sisters', the shell man snips out a bigger hole than their mouth, or whatever it is, and they are rather gritty. Then there will be a few clams, fat and crisp, and several of their little cousins, the *clovisses*. (When I am eating these sweet clams, I wonder why I think they are more delicious than any oyster . . . until I taste an oyster again!) There will be some *violets* in the *panaché*, unless one asks otherwise, and if I am alone I ask exactly that, for they are the one real disaster in the whole orderly chaos of Mediterranean sea life, for me at least. They seem like a mistake, somewhere along the path of natural creation. They are misshapen lumps of dun-colored spongy stuff, not shell, not skin, and inside they have a yellowish flesh, not sticky, not solid, not runny. People like them, and break open a *violet* and spoon or suck out the insides and smile. Like egg yolk but subtler, they say, and reach for another. I give away my share, if we are eating a *panaché* together, and slyly accept a clam or mussel in exchange. . . .

At most of the fish restaurants, there are little dingy shakers of vinegar for people who like it on shellfish, but I have never once seen anyone use it. In fact, most of the cut lemons on the shellfish seem to go back unsqueezed. Perhaps this is because the fish themselves are so succulent and cool and generally revivifying that nothing can make them better. They seem to breathe pure sea smell into the air, and to melt something of this same purity into their shells, to be drunk slowly, one long sip, after the meat has slid down our hot hungry gullets. It would be a pity to rush through such a salubrious inner bath as a platter of just-opened shellfish can give two-legged people, and a *panaché* needs a good half-hour of spaced concentration. Fortunately there are dozens of places in Marseille where this somewhat ritualistic enjoyment can be found and I know a lot of them, and by choice I would return without question to the 'Two Sisters', forever, or as long as they were there.

Once the two women are gone, the restaurant cannot possibly be the same, no matter how hard and well they have trained their relatives. They are as forceful as any females I have ever seen in a town well known for its ferociously strong ones, and I can well imagine them as young fish peddlers along the Quai des Belges, braying their strident quips to draw idlers and customers to their trays of the morning's catch. Possibly they worked along the sidewalk of the Rive Neuve, before they acquired the restaurant itself; they seem basically tough enough, even in their later years, to have stood up to the *entraîneuses'* dubious art of dragging clients into no matter how shoddy a fishhouse.

By the time I met them, more than twenty years ago, they looked as they still do: the younger one with dark hair and mocking but kind eyes, the older with grey-white hair and the almost benign face of a reliable client of Central Casting, always ready to play a gentle old granny, a saintlike elderly nun. Of the two women, I feel certain she is the tougher. Both of them seemed fed on tiger milk, and rubbed with a potent salve made by Artemis herself, of equal parts of olive oil, garlic, tomato paste, and rosé wine, blended with enough flesh of new sea urchins to make a thick paste. (When I have eaten with them, I feel as if some of it had been rubbed off on me. . . .) I can see them in bed making love and birthing children as easily as I can see them zipping through the restaurant from back kitchen to front glass door, watching every table, talking constantly.

There are always some waitresses and waiters to watch and supervise, or a *loup* to grill and flame, or a steaming bouillabaisse to serve in a storm of ladles-spoons-plates. People need to be seated, need more wine, need an extra pastry or a feast-day glass of cognac. The oyster man disappears into the back room for fresh supplies, and one of the Sisters opens mussels and clams twice as fast as he, while the other pulls a big lobster from the pile on top of the stand and holds it up triumphantly beside a table. "Look at its fat load of roe," she commands in a modified shriek, so that all the surrounding tables will fall silent to stare in awe. "What a superb female," she cries, whacking its belly casually, as if its claw were not reaching for any part of her to pinch, and then she runs toward the kitchen with it. Another group of clients stands up, and there is a rush for their coats, with both Sisters helping tuck them on like nannies with sated children. "Come back soon, come back," they call out onto the sidewalk, without losing a step in their routine dance.

And this goes on twice a day, six days a week. What we see is the top of the iceberg, as in any good restaurant. Beneath it is the real organization: the staff, both seen and invisible; the provisions, constantly checked and renewed; the upkeep of the whole small tight place, with all its linens, glasses, table fittings, and its essential fresh cleanliness. Above all, there is the skilled synthesis of fast and slow *people,* that they will work together on bad days and hectic festivals, through heat waves and the worst mistrals. (There is one niece or perhaps friend who is somewhat simple-minded, and who has been there as long as I can remember. She is unfailingly sweetfaced and attentive, and is very slow. One or the other of the Two Sisters is always nearby, watching to see if she needs a deft hand with the serving, never telling her to hurry. . . .) Such an operation lives or dies with the control of its leaders, in this case two women, and every time I return to its welcome hum and buzz, I know before even seeing them that both of them are there. I doubt that one could carry on without the other . . . run the joint so joyously, except perhaps by plain momentum for a time. When that wears off, weariness will settle like dust on the absorbed bright faces of all the relatives, and perhaps younger people will buy the restaurant, and perhaps it will stay a good one. Even in Marseille, though, the secret of Artemis' salve is not known to everyone, and the Two Sisters, changeless as they may seem, cannot live much longer than the rest of us. Selfishly, I hope it will be longer than I do. . . .

The Mediterranean has fed us for so long that it is unlikely even current human stupidities of pollution and destruction will stop its generosity. As we learn respect instead of carelessness, its fish will swim more healthily than ever, and its shells will form closer to the shorelines again, and the salt-sweet weeds will wave lushly for the picking. And meanwhile there will probably be places, as now, where we can smell the tonic freshness of a stand of mollusks on their cool grass, and choose a fish to be poached or broiled while we pick wee snails with a sharp pin from their shells. Even strangers in a port like Marseille will let their noses guide them to such pleasures, and I can think of at least four restaurants there, besides the comparatively "plain" fishhouse on the Rive Neuve, where I would gladly go tonight, tomorrow noon, this minute.

Two are very near the Two Sisters. The New York, on the Quai des Belges, is currently the most stylish place in town, and perhaps the most expensive, and its small but irresistible oyster stand (with a stalwart young sheller in fisherman's togs, of course) serves impeccably fresh Belons and even lesser breeds. They are fat, cool, and as crisp as lettuce. The mussels match them, and all the clams, and a *panaché* at the New York is impressively delicious and worth a leisurely period of serious demolition, as is any other dish there.

Then up from the Rive Neuve on an ugly little square is L'Oursin, a far cry in elegance from the New York's four forks and one star, and in fact not even noted in Michelin. It is primarily a shellfish store, with open crates out on the sidewalk and a long counter of them on one wall of the corridor toward the back, with a few small tables facing it. Busboys run in from nearby bars, and neighbor children come with plates to be covered with open juicy shells, and the oyster man is a busy fellow long after the day's stuff is delivered from La Criée.

The back of the store, past a table with an incongruous display of excellent fruit tarts, widens into a dark room that is still small, with a tiny bar in one corner and "rustic" checked cloths on the crowd of tables. There are three or four healthy young waiters and the elderly owner, all related to him and the oyster man and Madame the Cashier at her desk right by the door, and all in tight striped skivvies. They are quick and skillful, and concerned about whether the wine is right, the dish a success. The last time I was at L'Oursin I really did not like some mishmash of clams and mussels in a vaguely Espagnole sauce that the chef recommended, and when the waiter saw that I had abandoned it for part of my sister's *petite friture,* he was plainly upset. "It was well made," I said ambiguously, "but not to my taste." He frowned and sighed. "A pity," he said. "You should have told me sooner. . . ." (What would he have done but sigh sooner? It was I who had ordered the dish. . . .)

Most of the clients seem familiar to the place and the staff, and they eat gustily and talk and laugh. There is usually one solitary young man, never the same but always very well tailored, who eats and drinks with finicky savoir-faire and seems to be thinking about what to say later that afternoon to his divorce lawyer. Once one cried silently, without a sob or hiccup, through oysters, stuffed grilled *rouget,* and fresh strawberries, with a large bottle of the house's best Savoy wine, a coffee, and then a cognac. He never wiped his cheeks with his gleaming white handkerchief, or blew his nose. When he left, there were several dark stains on his pale grey flannel lapels, and I hoped they would not dry before he kept his appointment.

The smell of shells and breathing fish and seaweed is of course stronger at L'Oursin than at the New York, but it has the same vitality in small or large doses, and is probably best, sharpest, strongest, at a big serious fishhouse called Au Pescadou, out on the Place de Castellane where all the main banks seem to be.

The Pescadou is run by a very successful firm of wholesalers whose little refrigerator trucks supply fresh mollusks and fish to good restaurants and markets all over town. It is not cheap, and is well located to please people used to fine food and wines . . . mostly important-looking men at noon, with a few well-fed elderly women from the neighborhood's stylish apartment houses. The restaurant is big and functional, with no balderdash about cut flowers and so on. One enters it through a large dim cave, open from the street and lined with an astonishing display of all kinds of fish, some still flapping or scrabbling or writhing according to their build. This cave is a market as well as a heady invitation to the restaurant, and people study what to buy for lunch or dinner, and maids run in for three dozen oysters to be opened. There are piles of beautiful lemons. The oyster man works like lightning. Four bankers pick out a *loup*, and a busboy rushes it back to the kitchen.

Once inside the Pescadou, there seems to be an almost religious hush, unlike the buzz and laughter of any other big restaurant I know. The noise of the insane traffic around the carrefour of the Place de Castellane is muffled by the deep cave of the fish store, and the diners talk quietly, perhaps of great financial dealings, but more probably of the best way to poach a fish of over four pounds. Many people eat by themselves, looking pleasurably thoughtful but not sad, not crying. Of course there are shellfish on their seaweed or cooked in a dozen ways, but most people seem to eat fish there, very simply cooked, served with austere concentration by skillful waiters who seldom smile.

Almost as different from the Pescadou as L'Oursin is from the New York is a fourth Marseille fish place I would go to in a flash, Michel's out at the beginning of the J. F. Kennedy Corniche, along the wild coast toward Cassis and Toulon. It is always crowded, I think. The shellfish and all the dishes are excellent. Like the Pescadou, it is somewhat less expensive than the New York, much more so than L'Oursin or the Two Sisters. (All of them cost a lot, lately, anyway. . . .) Michel's is also called the Brasserie des Catalans, and has three forks and a star in Michelin, although it does not seem "elegant" to me. There is a well-stocked stand of fish and mollusks facing the corner door, and the bright narrow restaurant branches off to left and right of it. The décor, aside from the alternately snarling or twinkling sea outside, tends toward fishnets and their stuffed glaring catch, and incredible shells. The waiters are experienced, and in a reserved way kindly. People take the main course seriously at Michel's, and poke and finger the fish they will choose to be cooked, but there is certainly no hush there, and everyone talks and laughs a lot. As usual, the wines are well chosen for what they are drunk with, and they are drunk generously, as if something nice must be celebrated.

It is ridiculous to imply that the restaurants I myself would gladly go back to in Marseille, any time at all and the sooner the better, are preferable to a dozen, a hundred, others that anyone else might name and know. I happen to like some very much, to be eager to find their peers or even better, and to feel apprehensive about a couple that may disappear . . . and to be actively sad about several whose doors can never open again, for me or other strangers or, saddest of all, for the Marseillais who have known them.

Of course it is possible, although improbable, that the old restaurant at the corner of the Canebière on the Quai des Belges will rise from its present dismal ashes. Certainly the air there, always moving, forever braced with its own strange chemistry of salt, sea water, fish, wet shells opening and shutting, could make a phoenix out of any once-sensate thing. But there was one place on the Rive Neuve, in air almost as restorative, that died *dead* a few years ago. It was Surcouf, between the Criée and the strip of noisy little fishhouses, an oasis of elegance looking out blandly at the sleek yachts and sloops around their clubhouse. Affluent elderly Marseillais went there, and smartly dressed Parisians on their way to Cannes and Monaco, and stylish young men and girls taking

prospective relatives to a "correct" place to impress them.
The food was among the best of my life, and best served. It
seemed to leap from the sea to the plate, with one quick
pause in midair over the chef's enchanted kitchen. The
patronne was a very large soft woman, the antithesis of locals
like the Two Sisters. She was nice, in a *grande dame* way that
tagged her at once as from Bordeaux or Lyon or one of those
almost foreign places, and she liked my two little girls.

Another person at Surcouf who liked Anne and Mary was
the charming elderly barman, a White Russian left over from
Paris in the twenties. The first time we met him, the girls
were carrying two small dolls made by a Russian noble-
woman, that had been given to them by a rich friend when
they left California, and that acted as security blankets until
they understood the words flying all around them. The little
dolls were exquisitely dressed, that day in correct street clothes
no doubt, and the Russian recognized them at once as crea-
tions of the Countess So-and-so. Anne and Mary became
fairy creatures in return, bearing secret messages to him from
the past. It was delightful, and the dream went on for almost
two years. The girls continued to take the magic dolls to
Surcouf long after they felt silly about such childish things,
and I sipped dry champagne with the barman and then
watched my thriving daughters learn the difference between
a superb *bourride* and a merely excellent one. . . .

In about 1961 we found the restaurant closed. Madame had
died. Surcouf would open again in two weeks. We felt re-
luctant to go back, and it was months later when we telephoned for a table for four, for dinner, to celebrate a dear
friend's birthday. The place seemed dimmer, although it was
promisingly crowded. A new man was behind the bar, and our
Russian friend was headwaiter. He looked haggard, and
overdid his proprietary manners toward Anne and Mary, no

longer children. He seemed to want to impress the young ill-trained waiters, who were openly mocking of him and muttering rude things at his lordly ways. He almost frantically insisted that we order a *loup* grilled over fennel twigs, saying loudly that we had always loved it so much. The girls glanced at me: we had never once eaten it at Surcouf. That night we did, and we could rightly tell the Russian that it was supremely delicious. But we left in a quiet depression, feeling the desperate moist handclasp of our friend, trying not to hear the brash young waiters giggling behind his back.

I remembered a chill I had felt one day when I was waiting for the children to join me for lunch. Over a drink with Madame, I asked her why she had opened the front of the Surcouf onto the sidewalk to make a *café-terrasse*. It had been a disaster, she said. It attracted the wrong kind of people, low-class sightseers who wanted a beer and a view of the Port and no more. "But we must move with the times," she sighed. I felt upset and contradictory.

The next time we went to Marseille we could still see the vertical electric sign saying *Surcouf* from our hotel windows, but it hung over a nightclub called something like Le Wisky Boom Boom. By now the club is empty, and the sign is gone, as is Madame, as probably is the Russian, as are the Countess's little dolls. . . .

There were other places, far from phoenixlike. One was almost too sophisticated, the Campa. We went there now and then, for its beautiful service and stuffed mussels, pastries that sent the children into trance, and the walls covered with fragments of very old mirror, freckled, blotched, that made the dim room and all its elegant clientele into drifted attenuated sea plants in a deep pool. Then one night we led two hungry travellers to it, and not a soul was there except the crew of waiters standing like mummies inside the door. Most of the lights had been turned low. The headwaiter swam in from the kitchen before we turned tail, and implored us to come in, and flicked on lights.

We saw ourselves in countless dull blotched twisted mirrors. Two waiters revived, and almost overwhelmed us with their hysterical spate of vitality. Wine was brought in two silver buckets, the old-fashioned kind in rococo carved wooden stands. If there had been a small stringed orchestra asleep somewhere in a pantry, it would have been dusted off and propped up to play for us. We were served stuffed mussels, of course, and other local oddities like the dried roe called *poutargue*, and more that I've forgotten, all better than ever before. The evening turned to gold. We laughed and talked, and the maître d'hôtel and the young waiters grew pink and danced around us, and nobody else even opened the restaurant door. When we finally went happily away we knew it had been a special evening, and not long after that the girls and I went back and there were ugly boards crisscrossed over the door: "Permanently closed." Why? How had it been so impeccably organized for so long? Did someone die, or flee with the funds? Were all the worldly eaters extras in a film, or had we dreamed the whole thing?

Sometimes everything I remember so keenly about the old Mont Ventoux on the corner of the Canebière seems as unreal, now that I know it is gone or changed. I am almost afraid to find out if it will actually break out again from behind its present corset of high boards. I wonder if I'll ever be there, once more, to look down on the Old Port, and drain the shell of every oyster on my plate, and then perhaps eat a piece of orange tart. I wonder if I want to. It is tiring, sometimes, to play the phoenix . . . even in that salt-sweet air. Artemis, help me!

Chapter 8

THE

OPEN EYES

I

There are many people like me who believe firmly if somewhat incoherently that pockets on this planet are filled with
what humans have left behind them, both good and evil,
and that any such spiritual accumulation can stay there forever, past definition of such a stern word.

For some of us, it exists strongly in Stonehenge, for instance, and can be a bad or good experience, depending upon
one's ability to accept non-Christian logic. Almost as puzzling as Stonehenge, once in my life, were the front steps of
a small doleful cathedral in central France, where I soon
knew that it would be best for me to leave, rather than try
to locate my uneasiness of spirit.

Then there are kindlier and even restorative places, which
like the bad or merely disturbing ones influence people
whether or not they are aware of their vulnerability before
such old forces. The half-ruined garden in the Misión de

San Juan Capistrano in Southern California, as I knew it more than fifty years ago, was such a spot, in spite of its comparative youth, and I suspect that it still gives even casual tourists an extra gift of serenity, no matter how unexpected or unrecognized . . . and that the Franciscans may well have planted it there on ground that had been loved by the Indians long before.

But to counteract such good, there is another pocket of ageless influences that can affect most human beings dangerously, if they let it and even if they do not: the wild white crag of bauxite in southern France called Les Baux. It is clearly a menace to us because of the accumulation of vicious brutality that has gone on there from the first greedy prehistoric Baussenques, who lived only for money, to Wise Man Balthazar's ruthless descendants, who lived only for power won through the graces of his holy star with its sixteen rays.

There have always been sorceresses and female prophets in Les Baux, whether from Rome or Romany. The treacherous grottoes carved by wind and human greed are peopled by millions of bats, called the mosquitoes of Hell, and there are remote black antechambers for nightmares and exorcism, and long dangerous tunnels leading to the Phantoms' Cave, and finally the Place of the Black Beast Himself. There is a buried Moorish treasure, deep somewhere, too horrible to dare search out. A Golden Goat guards its keys, and often runs noisily through the narrow crooked paths of the fortress, kicking down obscene sexual symbols that crop up ceaselessly on the immense stones.

The Church has tried for several hundred years to dissipate this gathering of evil spirits in Les Baux, and in the end has got rid of all but one of its pagan ceremonies, so that the famous enactment on Christmas Eve of Christ's birth is a controlled gentle version fit for family viewing, complete with watered-down pre-Christian symbols, and pretty with traditional tunes from costumed piper and drummer.

And up on the wide meadow, so high above the Valley of the Rhône that often the sea is visible, near to the steep cliffs from which live captives used to be pitched by the descendants of St. Balthazar, there is a great cross, completely useless if it is meant to quell the incredible evil of the place, whose force has built up until now one wonders how it would be possible to live on that mighty rock, even as a guide or postcard seller . . . why the gentle little lamb (Lamb of God, in his cage blazing with lighted candles for the sacrifice), and the flower-hung powerful ram pulling him toward the altar to the tune of fife and drum . . . why they don't wither and die, each Christmas Eve. What would happen if the Church let them march straight out to the cross near the deadly cliffs, instead of only up the short nave of the chapel? Would the bats sing? Would the grottoes glow with their own answer to the holy candles?

Possibly not even an atomic bomb could unsettle, for very long, the collection of such an ancient mysterious mecca of damned souls. But of course not all the souls that have stayed in Les Baux have been damned, any more than all the people who built Stonehenge were filled with an awesome knowledge of celestial logic, or than the captive Indians who built San Juan Capistrano for their priestly invaders were filled with gratitude and joy. Both good and evil rimmed these receptacles perforce. Evil and good have been yeasts, bacilli, and one or the other has taken over, the way cancer or syphilis can either gain control of a human body or lurk in the shadows, held at bay by natural, spiritual, and even scientific forces.

The ancient port-city of Marseille, some fifty miles south of Les Baux, has a reputation for wickedness that is certainly wider spread than almost any other's in the world, partly because so many millions have passed through there and found what they were looking for, but unlike Les Baux, it seems to remain basically healthy. However, if one subscribes to the theory that some places collect curses or blessings as if they were pockets to be filled, buckets, vases, then it would be easy to blame the bad reputation of Marseille on some such thing as its three hundred years of building and servicing the galleys there and keeping them filled with slaves and criminals, most of them sending out great stinking auras of hatred.

The first galley made in France was toward the end of the fourteenth century in the Vieux Port, and it served as one of numberless fighting vessels built and docked in Marseille's shipyards. In 1385 the local fishermen outfitted one to protect their boats from pirates, and as the Church grew in strength, archbishops had their own escorts of slave-powered galleys, and carved saints rode every prow, from Michael to the Holy Sinner Magdalen. In 1533, for the marriage of Catherine de Médicis with the Duke of Orléans, there were eighteen royal galleys in port, and by 1696 Louis XIV kept forty-two galleys in Marseille waters, all outfitted and ready to fight.

The galleys designed and built in the great yards of the Vieux Port were called Marsilians, and were known wherever men rode the waves, for their two rudders and their catlike maneuverability. They could turn this way and that, and sneak up silently on any foe, for any prey.

These cats were manned by human beings who, if they were kept in good condition by their owners, could row six knots an hour through any tide or weather. And from an edict signed in 1564 by King Charles IX, they were either Frenchmen condemned to forced labor, or Mussulmen cap-

tured in war or bought as slaves, all called Turks but made
up of real Levantines, or Senegalese Blacks, or North African barbarians. Their average price was high, around four
hundred pounds, and they were bartered for, and traded, exactly as if they were precious silk or jute.

The Turks in Marseille were given their own mosque and
cemetery. To keep things decent, captured French slaves in
Constantinople also had a special chapel built for them.
Everything was fair and square, and the bills of lading read
like:

> Bought at Mallorca by order of Lord Beaufort:
> For 9 Turks: 6,453 pounds
> For Customs Duty: 645   "
> For Purchasing Agent: 32   "
> For Boarding-Vessel: 16   "
>
>   7,146 pounds
>
> Signed: Séguin, Consul

There was hateful rivalry between the costly Turks and
the cost-free French galley slaves, used cannily by their cap-
tains, of course, but little chance to express it. Mostly the
men lived and died on their benches, chained by one leg, and
wearing a gag around the neck that was ready to pop into the
mouth on order, to prevent talk and make the ears more alert
for commands. For a time all the slaves wore red caps like a
brand, but later they had none at all against the sun and
the sleet. Their officers were armed with a stick, a whip, and
a lash. . . .

If a man became patently useless at his oar, he could be
bought off: a Frenchman cost one high-placed purchase and
replacement, but a Turk needed two backers and then two
more Turks in his place. Madame de Sévigné more than
once finagled galley spots for troublesome young country-

men in the seventeenth century . . . much as reputable Americans bought positions for their unwanted siblings or enemies in both sides of the Civil War. This exchange solved unwelcome political, domestic, and perhaps financial problems, and the risk of a resentful or even murderous revenge was slight.

The galleys of Marseille were from the first a tourist attraction, and perhaps it was there and then that pocket-picking became an art that still thrives, I am told, in broad daylight along the Canebière, on the Cours Belsunce, in murkier corners. It is said, for instance, that one bishop went on board a new galley to give it and the slaves his official blessing, and announced that he defied any man there to take his wallet, but when he left he found that he was without the heavy gold episcopal cross worn around his neck.

Once in port, often three or four thousand slaves at a time were housed in enormous barracks at the southeast end of the little harbor, used also for shipbuilding, sword sharpening, and the countless parties so dear to the city: the men would shout huzzahs like trained seals at a given signal, raise their oars in forty galleys at a time before the City Hall for some visiting admiral or prince, and sit helplessly under thousands of paper lanterns on the brightened water, while people danced and bands played.

Louis XIV loved to make war, or at least to have a good force behind him in case things came to that point, and by the end of the seventeenth century Marseille was the hub of his fighting navy, for building, arming, and maintaining an astonishing fleet of the subtle, sneaky, Marsilian galleys. A new Arsenal was built, an engineering marvel, from its prison barracks and ironworks and road factories to the elegant Commanders' House, hung with Gobelin tapestries, a fine place for celebrating everything from the King's recovery from a head cold to the overnight stay of one of his grandchildren. Three balls could go on there at once, complete with specially written operas and great suppers.

There was a real hospital for the condemned men, however, in those grand days: six big wards for the Turks to one for the French. This practical as well as merciful provision came from a gentleman of Provence named Gaspard de Simiane-la-Coste, apparently the only such benefactor without a statue in that country given to their erection in any and every little park or cranny. Above the hospital wards was the armory, rising up in four galleries around a covered hall, and known to house the most beautiful war implements in the world. It was a sight to behold, and countless travellers did so, and there were grand parties, at which living tableaux were given to martial music, with symbolic representations of Louis XIV's might, ringed by kneeling Turks hung with golden chains that were exchanged for their own irons as soon as the shows were over.

The Arsenal was, well before 1700, a city in itself, and employed free men along with its forced labor. Some of the slaves were allowed to go outside, and gradually they built shacks across the Vieux Port where under constant guard they could carry on their old trades as tailors, toymakers, and weavers. Many more men were used as domestics by the officers and rich citizens. They were returned to the Arsenal at night, and any Marseillais who let one escape was fined the price of a new Turk.

Once, during the dreadful Plague of 1720, Marseille ran out of gravediggers, and on August 8, twenty-six Turks were put into service, with the promise of their liberty. Two days later, however, they were all dead. Fifty-three more, then eighty, then a hundred and another hundred men were sent into the nightmare around the Port. The job was to pick up the bodies, pile them onto carts, and dump them into the great ditches dug hastily for them. Twelve hundred people a day were dying, and on September 16 a brave gentleman named Roze commandeered enough galley slaves to clear a thousand cadavers off one of the quays, where they had lain for some three weeks, in less than half an hour. A commemorative plaque and a bust were erected to him. And back at the Arsenal, while only four men survived this forced service, the air was kept "perfumed" and most of the galleys were moved out of the Old Port, and of ten thousand slaves only about seven hundred died.

By the middle of the eighteenth century there were only eleven galleys left in Marseille, thanks largely to the fact that naval activities had been moved on down to Toulon and that slavery was beginning to seem "un-Christian." By 1784 the Arsenal had been sold by the King to outside speculators, since Marseille did not want to buy it, and only two galleys were left to be viewed by the tourists and then carted off. One of them, *La Patience*, served in the invasion of Egypt from Toulon in 1784, and was manned by free volunteers and then scrapped.

And by now nothing is left of the Arsenal . . . except that some people sense a pool of spiritual agony there where for hundreds of years men who had been ripped from their homelands by force, war, politics, must live and die chained to their oars or in their prison barracks. Up around the Opera, where the Hospital and Armory once stood, there are countless shady little hotels with their listless women waiting outside, and behind them rooms for shadier pleasures. Along the Rive Neuve, above the fish-bistros, there are "clubs" of varied repute, offering even more varied diversions to their members. Farther down toward the wholesale fish market, La Criée, and back of the waterfront, there are gathering places called names like the Galley Slave and the One-Eyed Pirate, where loops of tiny lightbulbs twinkle at odd hours, and sounds of bad dance-music seep up from the sidewalk, and some of the toughest girls I have ever seen lead young men toward the dark.

All of this is part of what was left by countless slaves who sweated blood and hatred and lust there. It will continue. A mysterious thing about Marseille, though, is that its collective evil is balanced by a wonderful healthiness. This too is what the galley slaves have left: the children they sowed in the sturdy stock of the Massilians, the children of Greek sailors from Phocea, and of wandering hardy tribes behind them, the prehistoric salt gatherers.

The reason, perhaps, for this balance of evil and good influences on the people of any such place is that it can be, as in Marseille, deeply religious.

It is "Christian" now, in the sense that this form of worship is the last manifestation of its ageless need for altars, altars behind altars, idols behind idols. It needs something to shout to and to dance around, to curse and to beseech, and because it is a natural gathering place on the globe for such human necessities, saints and sinners have collected there around the Vieux Port as irrevocably as water runs downhill.

When young Protis found himself married to the king's daughter and ruler of half the port-land, all in a few hours, he accepted the whole startling situation as a direct command of Artemis, the protector of sailors and therefore his own goddess. As soon as possible he built a temple to her, on the high northern hill above the city, and brought from Ephesus in Greece a handsome statue of her in her mummy-like wrappings covered with symbols and then her magnificent torso with its eighteen breasts in two vertical lines. She was accompanied by a famous priestess. A much simpler temple was built to Apollo, somewhat lower toward the sea, with its face looking out for mariners, but Artemis must face inland, to watch ferociously the creatures of the hunt, and to frighten off barbarians.

II

There is a saying, conveniently ascribed to the Chinese, that a temple should be built on a high breezy hill, within sound of water, and with a twisting path to dizzy and baffle evil spirits trying to assault it. Marseille's first two Grecian altars qualified in every way, and probably were built on other older worship grounds, because this rule is truly ancient. And since then Diana, the goddess of the hunt, took over from Mother Artemis, the fierce forest virgin, and after Diana came early Christian saints like Martha who survived the trip from Gethsemane to tame the great monster of Tarascon (somewhat after her natural time of death but legendary and therefore past chronology, and how else argue than historically with the great fire-breathing dragons that apparently peopled pre-Christian Provence?), and of course Mary Magdalen.

She was Artemisian, in her ability to survive the rigors of cave life in the bleak mountains east of Marseille, after she and Martha, and of course black Sarah, and dozens more saints, drifted to the local shores in a small rowboat piloted, some believe, by Joseph of Arimathaea, all nourished by one pot of chickpeas. The Holy Sinner, as she is now affectionately referred to, survived as well as Artemis could have in her dank cave, and baptized secret Christians for anywhere from twelve to forty years before she succumbed to what has been diagnosed by medical skeptics as chronic bronchitis.

As far as is known, she had only the normal allotment of breasts, but she nourished an uncommon lot of legends, and is still one of the leading and most subtly powerful citizens of Marseille and its environs.

And gradually statues of the Holy Mother Mary pushed out the earlier images of the huntress-goddesses, but usually on or near the same high airy sites. She grew softer, kinder, more gracious, as the Catholic Church changed God from cruel to loving, and the priestesses from avenging females of frightening power to innocent maidens.

And I became a friend of one, the little brown Virgin of the Abbey of St. Victor, below our apartment on the Rive Neuve side of the Vieux Port. I saw her often, because it was easy and easing to stop there on my way toward the Canebière or wherever.

She sat, about as big as a ten-year-old girl, in the catacombs that are constantly being excavated and opened under the massive fortlike church. She is made of walnut wood that has darkened since the end of the thirteenth century, when she was probably carved, and I do not know how or why she is there. There are ugly little replicas of her for sale at the bakery near St. Victor, which is famous locally for the *navettes* it makes all year round instead of only for her special week of celebration of Candlemas, La Chandeleur, on February 2.

That is when I first saw the little statue, enthroned to the left of the altar in the great abbey, almost hidden by layers of rich brocades and cloth of gold and gauzes of jeweled silver, her small head crowned with heavy flaming gems. The nave was filled with people, the whole place humming like a hive around its queen, all gently, all carrying slender green or green-and-white tapers. Hundreds were lighted, and there was a fine glow of them around Our-Lady-of-the-

Renewed-Flame, but most of the people bought them at the door to take home for a time of illness or disaster. Later I learned that the little brown Virgin is called on for help in times of trouble, and that she was brought out, for instance, in 1849, during an outbreak of cholera, and sat for some time beside the altar, offering whatever it was that she was being asked for. (I also learned that people who felt guilty about something used to go to the big door where the candles were sold during La Chandeleur, to smash their fingers under its heavy knocker as penance to her. . . .)

My own first meeting during the lighted celebration in 1973 passed without any requests from either of us, as far as I can tell. I did not buy a candle, although their slender fresh green pleased me. I stood here and there in the soft murmuring glow of the beautiful abbey, and liked the way people seemed somewhat shy but happy, and admired the jeweled doll.

During the next months, I ate a lot of *navettes*, little boat-shaped cookies, tough dough tasting vaguely of orange peel, smelling better than they are. They are supposed to symbolize the miraculous vessel Magdalen and all the other saints piloted to safety near Marseille. I did not much like the little pastries, but the bakery was run by some interesting ex-vaudevillians, and in one window were two sizes of the ugly plaster copy of the brown Virgin. I deliberated for almost four months about buying the small one to give to a Christian friend, but I never did. Now I am sorry. But it was too ugly, when I could go down into the grotto chapel and look at her: no jewels, no glittering capes, no glowing green candles, but still a steadfast emanation of health and simplicity flowing from the small wooden image.

It is difficult to understand *why* this goddess has been a solace to the Marseillais in bad times, but there is no doubt that she possesses an ageless serenity, and sends out a balm of renewal. The abbey where she stays, named St. Victor for the city's prime Christian martyr, was first built in about A.D. 400 on the site of the old Greek cemetery, across the Port from the beautiful temples where life was worshiped instead of death. When, and why, did the new small idol come to this gathering place of earthly sorrows to give help?

I I I

It is often hard to admit to the awareness of what is mysterious. I found it painful, when I went back alone to Marseille in about 1970, to acknowledge that I felt an almost physical dislike of Notre Dame de la Garde, the Old Gold Lady up on the hill, the Good Mother of all navigators. I returned to her church many times, to try to understand what had happened to my respect and acceptance of her as intrinsic to the religious sanity of Marseille, and in 1976, riding on a bus toward the Vieux Port from Aix, I suddenly understood it very clearly.

There is one point on the route where for a flash the distant unreal golden statue can be as sharp and in a strange way as heart-lifting as the sound of a trumpet. In the fifties and sixties, my children and I would wait for it, stop talk, fix our eyes on the special spot in time and space. And there she would be. And we would know we were almost on the Vieux Port again. We felt safe.

There was another small moment of excitement, of fulfillment, from the train, whether we took the local from Aix or rode the Mistral down from Paris or Dijon. We knew when to wait for it, prepare ourselves, and then suddenly *see* that gleaming Lady, tiny as a pinprick but mighty, towering over the town. We were almost on the Vieux Port again. We felt safe . . . *again!*

Soon, that day, certainly before we went back again to Aix, we would go up to the church. We walked, or now and then took a cab, to the peculiar hydraulic elevator that has since been condemned. It ran by water which gushed dramatically at the bottom as the wobbly little cage rose slowly to the top of its slightly slanting tower, and most of the passengers were plainly frightened by the strange ascent, no matter how often they had made it. My older girl always closed her eyes until we jolted to a halt, and while I never felt anything but a fatalistic curiosity about the little flight, it was good to step out of the cage onto the long high bridge that connected the elevator tower to the mountain itself. Far below us were rooftops and then, on down to portside, the crowded quarters of the Rive Neuve. It seemed as if we could see forever, but we always hurried, because we knew that once we were on the mountain, once we had climbed the hundreds of stairs up to the church, the puny bridge and its little views would lose all their first excitement by comparison with what we had there.

We could walk clear around the huge ugly basilica, and look in every direction of the compass, from its great terraces and ramparts. Sometimes we held on to each other, to feel safer when the wind blew. Usually we climbed up to the east bastion of the fortress that the church is built on, where it juts out like a gigantic stone ship's prow. A flat round table, set with a map in mosaic, told us what we were seeing: city, Vieux Port, the Mediterranean, all the islands . . . we never tired of looking at it, and never felt dizzy, because the fortress was so mighty and so safe.

All this, though, was simply a ritual, almost dutifully performed before the real reason for our countless visits to the mountain: the *inside*, inside, first the low dim crypt, then the light-blazing basilica above it.

It sounds sacrilegious, perhaps, to say that it was an enchanted palace, part of fairyland, but in the best sense that was so. The outside of Notre Dame de la Garde is awesome, with its drawbridge, its bastions, but it is also stark, and in a controlled way, savage. There are still pits in its walls from its last bloody siege, when the Germans held it before it was freed in August of 1944 by the Third African Division of the French Army. But underneath those new scars, for hundreds of years, are the ghosts of revolutions and mutinies and imprisonments and treacheries, and it can never be anything but frightening, even in the blazing sunlight of Provence.

The crypt, then, is like a low dark cave at first. It is enormous, the size of the church above it, but with a womblike reassurance, and gradually the soft lights in the little side chapels, and the glow of candles, make it come into focus like a murmurous dream. There have always been people there when we were, kneeling, wandering quietly from one chapel to another to look at the countless votive pictures and tablets and medals and miraculously useless crutches. Everything praises the miraculous, of course: the watchful defense of sailors first, then all travellers, and then the sick and otherwise endangered, by Our Lady of Protection, who in one form or another has stood on that steep rock for thousands of years, to guide and reassure.

It is impossible not to feel, there, something strong and trusting about the human spirit, and my girls and I accepted it wordlessly as we looked at crude little paintings of shipwrecks, and read quaint impressive poems of gratitude from sailors or their families whose prayers had been answered.

I think there is an elevator inside the church, probably for infirm visitors, but we were neither hobbled nor newcomers to the place, and it was fine to leave the softly dim crypt and walk up the great outer stairs to the basilica itself. We knew what would happen. It always did. Once inside, the place seemed to explode with light and color and rich crazy beauty. It scintillated. It was gay and lightsome. We gasped, and entered with a familiar feeling of delight.

The walls are made of many colors of stone, brought from wherever marble turns rosy or yellow, wherever any rock can be quarried that is green or blue or red, veined or pure. The ceilings of all the side chapels, of the dome above the main altar, of the nave, are mosaics brightly paved with gold. Their arches are supported by angels and archangels. The floor too is a brilliant mosaic carpet. The windows are like crystal, to make all the surfaces glint and gleam.

Above the altar there is the tall Virgin and Child in silver, sometimes crowned with gold and diamonds. They used to be carried in pilgrimages through the town, and once after the Revolution in the eighteenth century she wore a tricolor scarf on her head and the Child a little Phrygian cap, I have been told. . . . There is a lot of lapis lazuli, as I remember, and above the altar are two astonishing lamps of silver. It is all heartwarmingly, generously vulgar.

And the best part, of course, is what countless Christians have brought to Notre Dame, to recall their gratefulness. Their *ex voto*s hang from the high vault of the nave on cords or perhaps wires that are almost invisible, but that are symbolical of the connection between earth and heaven, and they twirl a little sometimes, very slowly, if there are crowds beneath, or if the mistral is strong outside. There are little whittled rowboats once brightly painted, and dime-store battleships; there are life rafts and plastic toy submarines and a few streetcars and many airplanes. There is at least one World War II tank, I remember, and a toy ambulance, and my younger daughter swears there is a very small baby buggy.

A lot of the side chapels are dedicated to martial miracles: sailors, regiments, generals, admirals. There are little marble plaques from famous soldiers, dedicated to Our Lady for saving them from long-forgotten battles on such-and-such a date. There are a lot of medals and epaulettes and swords.

The fine excitement of the whole place, though, comes from the hundreds of subtly moving votive images on their long strings, tiny in the dazzling rich colors of the church, all there because men prayed and were saved to live a little longer. The odor of thanksgiving is strong, from all these devout emotional symbols, and it is extremely innocent and direct.

My children and I always absorbed it as simply as we breathed the heady salt air of Marseille, and almost romped down the old winding path past the oratories where pilgrims could stop to pray and catch their breath, with a new feeling of life. Once back on the Rive Neuve we took the little ferry across to the Quai du Port, and stood in front of the lovely Town Hall and looked across at Our Guardian Lady. There she was, straight as a flame on the high belltower above the church, above the old fortress, on the sharp mountain above the town and the port and the sea. We were safe.

There were the requisites of the Chinese dictum: temple on high hill, winding path to baffle evil spirits, sound of water . . . if not the rush of the old hydraulic elevator, the plash of *l'eau bénite* in generous basins for the believers . . . so, what happened to make me feel sour and resentful a few years later?

I went back automatically, and things seemed drab and cold. There were busloads of tired lumpy tourists. There were gift shops and snack bars. Worst of all, there were printed signs everywhere, telling me in four languages not to do this, to do that, to keep quiet, to be respectful, to remember that I was in a holy place, and most of all that this holy place did not in *any* way belong to the city of Marseille but to the Church in *every* way, at *all* times. . . .

The signs were what turned the trick. They were even inside the entrance to the crypt and the nave: Pray! Silence! Be Reverent! . . . and they still were there when I went back in 1976 to see if what I discovered on the bus was true. It was: I had lost the innocence, the feeling of mystery that was so strong when I was with my children.

I was alone. I felt everything as a weary cynical observer, not as a delighted excited new soul. The beautiful mosaics looked coarse. The silver lamps and Mother and Child were vulgar. The votive ships and submarines and tanks seemed foolish and dusty. And the signs . . . they were insulting, and I felt trouble in them: someday the Marseillais would take things into their own hands, as they had done before, and heads would roll, and the drawbridge would be pulled up in another siege . . . and the reason I was so dour, I saw in a flash as I looked automatically at the precise point in the bus trip across to the far flash of Notre Dame de la Garde, was that I had let myself lose the innocence my little girls had loaned to me. I felt ashamed and sad.

So I went to stand in front of the Town Hall. And there she was! Across the crowded waters of the Vieux Port, high as the sky, golden in the sunlight, the colossal statue seemed to ride the basilica, the fortress, the crag, the city itself, as if she were the figurehead of a ship forever safe from danger. I knew that at night she would be lighted, a symbol to tired travellers and the ships at sea, and that the grave sound of her mighty bell would ring for them, for me.

I knew many other things; the statue is more than forty feet tall, made of an alloy of copper and zinc in four hollow sections, with a circular staircase inside so that there is a bird's view of Marseille through the eyes of her somewhat pudgy face. She was put into place in 1870, and the deep-toned bell was christened Marie-Joséphine and first rung in 1845. It was made in Lyon, shipped down the Rhône to Avignon, dragged by relays of Percheron horse teams toward the mountain, and then up. I know about some of the countless pagan-Christian pilgrimages, and royal luncheon parties after Mass, and desperate prayers during the Plague of 1720 and the cholera epidemic in the nineteenth century. The first gift to the church was a little sack of coins from Gilbert des Baux, one of the descendants of Wise Man Balthazar . . . but the second was a liter of olive oil from a nameless work-man. Then pearls and gold flowed in. . . .

I knew, too, that after Julius Caesar crossed the Rubicon in 49 B.C. and destroyed Marseille to spite Pompey, he built a temple to Vesta or perhaps Ceres on the mountain, to show his gratitude for being so powerful. And before that, the Phoenicians worshiped Baal Milkarth there. And of course the Phoceans had a temple to Artemis there as well as across the Port, where later Diana and Apollo were worshiped on the gentler hills. I knew how the high peak has for unknown centuries been a watchtower, a chapel, a fort, sometimes all together. And the garish richness inside, the ugly striped architecture outside, the cruel ramparts and staircases with their insolent signs, became completely unimportant as I took a new long look. They were almost as evanescent in Time as I myself was, but they had, through the innocence of my children, taught me how to be aware of man's trust, even if my own seemed occasionally to weaken and falter.

Albert Einstein wrote, "The most beautiful thing we can

experience is the mysterious . . . the source of all true art and science. He to whom this emotion is a stranger, who can no longer pause to wonder and stand rapt in awe, is as good as dead; his eyes are closed. To know that what is impenetrable to us really exists . . . this knowledge, this feeling, is the center of true religiousness."

Marseille is not a stranger to this awe, and its eyes have never closed.

Chapter 9

SOME
DIFFERENCES

The differences between a *fête* and a *foire*, in Marseille, are cold and clear, but the two are as apart-alike as breathing in and then out, in a healthy body.

A *fête* is a celebration of something. It can be a public holiday ordered by Church or State and printed on calendars: Christmas, July 14, All Saints' Day. It can be a family anniversary, a birthday, printed in private memories. It can be like the day in February when people walk to St. Victor to buy a green taper for Candlemas, either to light bemusedly in the murmurous abbey or to carry home for possible succor in case of death or rheumatism.

A *fête* can be solemn and quiet or unbelievably noisy, but a *foire* is noisy perforce, and often garish or giddy as well as commercial in one way or another. It is a big organized carnival, no matter how decorous its motives. People will come to it from everywhere, in summer yachts or winter caravans, and sailors to it will sleep in their chosen ways all around the Vieux Port, as will artisans and their wives

during the Foire aux Santons up along the Allées at the top
of the Canebière . . . and then the garlic merchants, and the
nursery garden growers, and the land developers. . . .

Kings, bishops, the Chamber of Commerce, and other rep-
resentatives of earthly power have officially organized fairs
in Marseille since August 19, 1318, when Robert of Provence
authorized a three-day celebration in honor of his dead
brother, St. Louis of Anjou. Louis, who had been Bishop of
Toulouse, was buried in the Franciscan Convent in Marseille, and for reasons best known to King Robert and probably his astrologers, it seemed a judicious time to give the
populace a little diversion . . . dancing, free food for the
lucky, pomp and paradings.

Fairs are far from coincidental, politically or otherwise,
with the conjunction of stars and human yearnings. Long
before Rome, it has been a truism that if subjects seem to be
growing fractious, hot-blooded, or otherwise lunatic, a good
circus is indicated. If garlic, onions, and herbs are ready to
be used, let people flock to town to buy them and then spend
money in the public houses as well as the crowded merry
streets lined with booths. If the sun is high, let amateur sailors be invited to crowd the bright blue port with their pretty
barks, and then fill all the quays with their tanned thirsty
gaiety. And if the future looks grim, no matter how short it
may be (Lent used to be a good example of this limited
period of self-denial), let there be a good carnival first, to
ease the body and give due cause for remorse (with the
primeval rewards of springtime after the dark days . . .).

When Protis sailed into the Vieux Port to buy salt some
twenty-six hundred years ago, he unwittingly crashed a party
that some observers feel has never really stopped. The King's
daughter chose him in marriage that first night, by raising her
wine glass to the young Greek captain, and wine is still as

much a part of life there as is water, or the celebration of turning one into the other, although there is little drunkenness in this ageless miracle, among the natives.

The first Massilia, now one of the world's richest, most devil-ridden and exciting ports, seems to live in and for a constant calendar of festivities and rites, and a full enjoyment of whatever they offer. Except for the slight inconvenience of having to get back to work on Monday morning when the whistle blows, Sunday night is as long and lovely as Saturday. Weekends as well as fairs and all such celebrations are made for pleasure and relaxation, and it is a poor stick of a Puritan from Dijon or Paris, or even Chicago or Munich, who cuts short the obvious delights of a pleasant evening simply because tomorrow means work.

The same is true of any holiday in Marseille. It lasts longer, is noisier, and in general seems like more fun than in any place else in the world. New Year's Eve, for instance: in my own experience, it starts about two hours before midnight on December 31, on the Vieux Port anyway, and lasts until the last feeble toot of a taxi horn at three the next afternoon.

It begins with horns, too, and increasingly they include happy-sounding cornets, trombones, even saxophones, and all kinds of whistles, blown from the windows of every moving car, and from ambling groups on all the sidewalks. At midnight, of course, there is a splendid ritual of sound, and all the bells ring above the burst of noise from ground level, with the grave tone from Notre Dame de la Garde holding them together. Guns and other explosives crackle, and there are wild yells and screams, and sirens. And the most astonishing thing about this deliberate abandon is that its conventional salute to the New Year does not cease with the pealing bells and the singing of "Auld Lang Syne," but is as savage at three and then five and even eight in the morning as it was at midnight.

I listened to it once from the top floor of the Hotel Beauvau, and although I never slept a minute of that night, I felt afterward as if I had been cleansed and refreshed by the virile strength of the sound, which seemed as if it would never stop, and rose in a subtly wavering roar to my windows. Now and then I would look down at the Quai des Belges, bright as day under the elaborate civic decorations of great dolphins and starfish made of colored lights, and cars would be moving with slow skill, sometimes with somebody like a white-haired man alone on the top playing a trumpet, other times bursting with wild-eyed girls in vivid silks, singing. I would go back to my bed again, rocked in a more pagan rhythm than ever before or since.

By nightfall of that New Year's Day, Marseille was as quiet as a church. An occasional empty bus moved along the silent streets. Most of the restaurants and cafés were closed, or kept dimly lighted by one semiconscious waiter who complied with the unwritten law about maintaining refuge for weary travellers. . . . All the stores were dark. It was eerie to walk along the Canebière and not meet even a dog. There was no sign of the sixteen hours or so of celebrating: no broken glass or dirty confetti, no vomit against a wall. The Marseillais had greeted the new year as they felt it to be fitting, drunk on their own love of any excuse for a party, and strong enough to make it perforce the noisiest, longest one ever given, at least since the year before. There was no citywide hangover, as would seem indicated after such a rout, but only an innocent need for sleep and silence.

By the next morning the fishwives were sharp-eyed behind their trays of flopping catch along the Quai des Belges, the shops everywhere were bustling, the banks were sedately busy. . . .

There are, of course, official holidays besides New Year's Day, such as Christmas, May the 1st, Bastille Day. This somewhat rigidly dictated list does not daunt the Marseillais, however, for there are always the *foires*. There is a Spring Fair, complete with day-and-night displays and contests for everything from swimming to hairdressing, and from judo-for-ladies to the filleting of fresh sardines. Somewhere along in here comes the International Sailing Week, when the Vieux Port is filled with elegant vessels of every size, and the pubs hum with bronzed, hungry yachtsmen and their ladies, all speaking twenty tongues.

Easter is in the *fête-foire* pattern too, in a city that has fought fiercely for Christianity since its first martyrs, after Mary Magdalen preached there on the porch of the temple of Athena (and left her brother Lazarus to be the town's first Bishop), a city that is willing to accept its present Communism for any good excuse to decorate the altars, and then dance to the gods and goddesses that were behind them first: Apollo, Artemis . . . further back.

In midsummer, there is the Garlic Fair, which until lately, when it was moved to a nearby area, was held at the top of the Canebière, around the handsome old bandstand and down the shady Allées where, two days a week in almost every weather, is one of the most beautiful flower markets in the world. The air is as heavy as ozone there, on Tuesdays and Saturdays, and so purified by the thousands of potted and cut blossoms that it seems improbable any odor could attack it, from the gassy vehicles pouring up and down the wide street . . . except in midsummer, of course, when over that whole part of the city there floats from the Fair the scent of freshly gathered garlic.

It hangs in short braids, or loops in long heavy cables from all the stands that spring up in a few hours. It spills from the backs of parked trucks and wagons. It lies in piles on canvas spread on the sidewalks, and there are nutlike sacks of it as tall as a man. Housewives pinch and sniff and fill their baskets for storage; buyers for big hotels and restaurants in Provence sample freely as they make out their orders; wholesalers from half of Europe compare lots and bargain with the farmers. It is exciting, and a handsome scene, with the silky glistening garlic everywhere, to look at and to breathe. Some men in Provence say their women are beautiful because of garlic, and some women say their babies are healthy because of it, and their men stronger than other men.

There is another International Fair in September, complete with exhibits, contests, booths, flags, the general commercialized hoopla. But the next time the real stands go up, at the top of the flowery Allées, the trees are bare, and will stay that way until the last stall is empty, and then well past that. The famous Foire aux Santons begins on the first Sunday in December, and with luck, or perhaps the contrary, a few booths will still be open in mid-January, shielding what is left of the stock of little clay figures piled on the rickety counters, half-priced, with the boss or his indomitable wife sleeping on a cot behind a flap of canvas as nightwatchers of the leftover crumbs.

At the start of the Fair, it is a different picture. The Allées are lined on both sides with dozens of booths, brightly painted and as brightly lighted in the quick wintry twilights and then the chill nights, and the wide sidewalk between them is jammed with people, pushing and gaping and joking with the vitality that I believe is peculiar to Marseille. It is like the midway of a carnival but more intense, less fragmented, of course with loudspeakers blaring above the human sounds in this age. There is a general air of animal enjoyment, and cafés do a land-office business, and it is all (at least for now) because thousands of painted figurines can be looked at and compared, and bought, to depict the birth of Jesus Christ.

The images, not all of little saints as their name would imply, come in several heights, set rigidly by the Guild of Santonmakers, with the tiniest called "fleas," and the biggest perhaps a meter high, and in spite of personal quirks of the artists who produce them, they are endearingly alike.

How could the story be changed? Everybody in Provence knows that the Baby was born in a stable, so there is a Provençal cowshed, with straw laid on the floor for a bed. Sometimes the straw is real, for an expensively large image, and sometimes it is a tiny blob of yellow plaster for one of the minute crêches that are fitted into halved walnut shells and still sold by the less famous *santonniers*, the ones with wives and small children willing to help paint them when the season is slack. The Baby always wears a decorous white shirt, and is pink in the face. His Mother and Father never change either. How could they dare to? She wears blue and looks beatific, and he wears a brown cape and looks bewildered.

There are the Ox, the Ass, and the Three Wise Men. And then there are the other people who came to worship, that night in the village in Provence: the Shepherds who saw Balthazar's star, the Fisherman and his catch, the Laundress with her basket of clean linens, the Mayor and his Wife, the Miller with a sack of flour, the evil Gypsy, and all dressed in the village clothes and country capes and boots of the early nineteenth century, when the play that tells about this great event first took shape. In one form or another, it is always called *La Pastorale*, and it still plays all through the region, well past Christmas itself: a cast of dozens of local people and animals, held more or less in line by two or three roving professionals: very broad humor, good fife-and-drum music, hearty dancing, local jokes, everything sung and spoken in Provençale. The audience knows every line, and often has a child or newborn lamb in the cast, and the women wear old family costumes oftener than stylish holiday clothes. The show is hours long, with a merciful break half through it.

The story is about a quarrelsome village, miraculously united by the birth of a little stranger in a cowshed, and it is even more familiar than our Red Riding Hood or Mickey Mouse, and the *santons* repeat its simple legend meticulously, to a knowing and basically pagan audience. The Mayor must wear his black silk top hat and the Fishwife carry her brass scales, and the Virgin be in blue, no matter what hands (Gypsy? Communist? Muslim?) have shaped and painted the little figures.

Tradition steps aside for the extras, though: hens and their chicks, and Provençal windmills and cypress trees and a bridge for the boy angler, and dogs and lambs and a donkey to help the woodcutter. They are irresistible, and the tinier they are, the more the fairgoers seem to want them, to put in their pockets and take home for a family Nativity.

The first time I saw the Foire aux Santons it was at its peak of excitement, the second Sunday in December. Thousands of people joined the slow march up and down the Allées, gaping, stopping to buy, eating hot sugared peanuts from the little stoves that smoked here and there into the cold air. The last time was well after the holidays, and most of the stalls were gone or boarded up. Two or three stayed open to sell their remainders, the chipped or misshapen or mismated *santons* that nobody had wanted: a six-centimeter

Mary and a two-centimeter Joseph, a Baby with one arm gone.

It was a *foire* I went to, then and often in Marseille. It was as commercial as the Summer Regattas I looked down to in the Vieux Port, when it was a solid flicker of bright sails heading for the open sea. All the fairs were planned, perhaps contrived by both stars and men, to bring people together when the planets gave them the right indications of harvest, high sun, rebirth. So it may be that they were *fêtes* too, ageless celebrations of life.

Chapter 10

MAY DAY,
1932–73

May Day is taken seriously in Marseille, a solid Socialist-Communist stronghold. It is firmly and almost solemnly a breather for the hard workers: stevedores, shipbuilders, construction men . . . and few women are seen in the cafés and on the quays of the Vieux Port, even if they are breadwinners in their own right.

Some of the better-class restaurants close, ostensibly to give their staffs a free day but really because the people amiably monopolizing the sidewalks would never set foot over an elegant threshold, for both financial and ideological reasons. On the other hand, the pubs and bistros are open and crowded from early on the Great Day until the last dog dies. Usually the weather is benign, and little round tables push almost over the curbs.

The older men look shaved and rather formal under their Sunday hats as they saunter along, their eyes out for old pals, fellow welders or carpenters they may not have seen since that big job in '54 or '62. They meet, greet, sit talking for a

time, and then roam on, drinking sagely in the face of a
hundred other such encounters before nightfall. The younger
men, more casually dressed but as carefully, are hatless. They
make a formless parade of parental dignity and pride, with
one or two small children wearing their starched and frilly
best, tiny girls riding their fathers' shoulders, boys old
enough to walk keeping step, three to one, alongside. There
is not a pram or baby-pusher in sight: plainly a woman's
symbol, and not manly enough for this annual display of
virility and fatherly tenderness. There is much handshaking
and comparing of progeny, on the wide sidewalks, and hundreds of children peck politely at their tenth or twentieth ice
cream or orange soda while their fathers talk shop over
their small glasses of *pastis*.

The sounds are good, from thousands of male voices
laughing and gabbling in the sunny air. The traffic is not
heavy, since a lot of the buses are laid off and there are few
taxis. The port looks strange without its rickrack in the
wakes of the two little ferries, firmly tied up for the Day at
their berth on the Rive Neuve. The fishhouses on that side
do a long steady business, of course, mostly for groups of
three or more men eating oysters to prove that at least once
or twice a year money means nothing to them, or ordering a
magisterial bouillabaisse to prove that they are genuine citizens of the town. The young fathers wander up the Canebière to the Place St. Louis or the Cours Belsunce, where they
buy snacks for the children from the open booths and sit
under the softly leafing plane trees with a few buddies, before they head home for the special meal the wives have made
during their "free" day without all the kids underfoot.

There is a haunting air about the First of May, aside of
course from the obvious ceremonies that have been carried
out rather summarily in various working quarters and big

meeting places: oratory, discreet police surveillance, a flourish
of trumpets now and then. All that must of course be got
through, a token, a symbol. But what the men wait for is to
wander in the sunlight, once their comradely duty has been
done, and be free, free for a day that without the Revolution
would mean routine work. They want to show off their little
children, and encounter hit-or-miss their peers, and drink a
few *pastis* without pressure from either women or clocks.
There are no bosses, in other words, on May Day. It is the
workers' own, hard fought for and hard won and to be
savored to the hilt, by men who may never have tasted revolution itself, but who know why it has occasionally been
indicated as necessary to the laboring masses.

On May 2 the dream will be over. On May 1 it is something to hang on to, and in the dancing sunlight around the
Vieux Port, that is easy. Toward evening the little children
sleep in their fathers' arms, or on benches anywhere, and
gradually the young men gather them up and walk slowly
toward their flats, while the older ones sit longer with a few
friends and start a lazy game of cards. In the outskirts of the
big city the day-long click of the *boule* balls grows still, and
lights go off early everywhere, if men must be up for the first
shift at the yards, the depots, the high-rise construction going
on near the new university. Sidewalk snack wagons and the
little restaurants around the Vieux Port put up their shutters,
and gradually the fishing boats ready themselves for whatever will be needed to assault whatever schools of fish may
swim on May 2.

So . . . May Day can be peaceable, as it seemed in Marseille
in 1973 and may still stay, far removed from its bloody be-
ginnings and from the social convulsions of the past decades.
The workers of the world, at least in that old southern port,
arise and after dutiful meetings to prove their unity they

wander with proud but relaxed freedom through the suddenly quiet streets of their town.

When I was first in Marseille on a May Day, in 1932, I
think, things were more tense, and less firmly controlled by
the people. The streets were almost silent, not filled with relaxed roamers as I saw them forty years later, but with occasional small groups of truculent-looking men who slid off
when the cops, always in twos, came into view. Of course
banks, post offices, schools, and most stores were tightly
closed, and then as in 1973 the only things kept open seemed
to be the cafés and the emergency rooms at the Hôtel Dieu
and some outlying hospitals . . . and of course the police
stations.

My husband and young sister Norah and I were there to
board an Italian freighter for San Pedro in California. It
seemed strange then and by now even stranger that the tub
would sail that special day, and that we three would be
there on time, drifting around the Vieux Port in a contained
anguish at having to leave the country, the language. We
were subtly catatonic, each in our own way, perhaps a little
drunk on white wine and regret.

As I remember it, our favorite hotel, called the Good Old
Beauvau in our private vocabulary then as now, housed a
restaurant on the corner of the Canebière and the Quai des
Belges, called the Mont Ventoux or perhaps the Beauvau–
Mont Ventoux. And as I remember it, there was an upstairs
dining room, above the sidewalk brasserie, with an open
balcony. And one went up to it from the Quai instead, as
later, by a plushy stairway leading off the main street. I even
think that I remember vines or green leaves shading the balcony tables, but this may be the influence of old postcards
and novels and research volumes bought but seldom con-
sulted. According to a 1939 Michelin it was run by M. Sicard

then, and probably was a few years before, when he almost threw me out of his restaurant.

We had done the best we could about seeing that our big wicker trunks were properly at the right dock, and had gone into one open record shop along the silent Canebière and one circumspect pharmacy on a side street, and after a drink in the kind of bar that fell quiet when we came in, we sagged disconsolate but undaunted toward the stairs of the Mont Ventoux.

Halfway up, the owner came hurrying down to us. Plainly he was tense and alerted to possible May Day difficulties, and over my shoulder I wore a small accordion that I had bought to fill the hours in a hotel room while my husband (in the University of Strasbourg's quieter library) changed a comma to a semicolon and then back again in his doctor's thesis. And M. Sicard said, with forceful clarity, *"Out! No beggars or street musicians! OUT!"*

What we did next apparently melted his heart, for we stood there like children to confess that we were sailing from Marseille in about two hours and that the accordion was for the long voyage, but that we *must* eat one more good meal on the Vieux Port. His eyes in a trained flicker appraised our shoes and hair, and with a cautious bow he led us to exactly the table we wanted, next to the balcony on the corner of the Quai and the Canebière. (Was there really such a balcony then? Was there a velvet hand in a steel glove named Sicard? Were we there at all?) We spent more than three hours eating and drinking, and knew tacitly that we were like people hoping vainly to be snowbound in a snug mountain cabin. Perhaps the freighter had already sailed . . . the snow would be too deep for a rescue. . . .

As we broke from the dream and started sheepishly to push back our chairs, the dragon-boss came toward us with a big dusty bottle and four balloon glasses, poured a family elixir distilled somewhere behind Cassis, and sat down firmly to share it. He was full of gallant chuckles about mistaking me for a street musician. We told him all kinds of winy nothings about being students in cold northern hinterlands like Dijon and Strasbourg, which he recognized to be French but plainly felt were as dismissable as Kanchatka or Popocatepetl. He told us of his farm and vineyard and family. We exchanged addresses. We told him about finding an open record shop, and he said it was a dangerous day, and then we said we hated violently to leave France and Marseille and the Mont Ventoux and him.

Suddenly he became alarmed, and with drastic assistance from what staff he could drum up at that hour he located a friend of a friend of a waiter who grudgingly agreed to drive a crony's cab to the Joliette docks. "It will cost somewhat more today," our new friend murmured, and then shouted impressively, "All speed! This is a life-and-death matter! Goodbye, goodbye. . . ."

It was May Day, the driver's day, and he hated capitalists, especially American tycoons who travelled selfishly on luxury liners and knew nothing of the hell working people lived in to serve them like slaves. He was a small rat of a man, filled with phrases, and as steeped in his own libations as we were numbed by the mysterious brew from behind Cassis, and his colossal grouch seemed both logical and familiar to us, headed as we were toward farther shores. We agreed to all of it, fatly fed and wined, as we bumped furiously and erratically toward our pier and one of the most evil little ships of my long life with and on them. (We three were one-third of the passengers, all neurotics, and the officers were more off focus than any of us, despairing rejects of the military system in their country. Their pathetic little Italian vessel was later to

be sunk as the first one tagged by the British in World War
II . . . a quasi-noble if overly delayed demise.)

On the way to this climax or dénouement or whatever it
proved to be in our high lonely day in Marseille on May 1,
1932, we sat for a timeless time in the steaming taxi while
a surprising number of armed cops on the dock and up on
deck blew whistles and yelled wildly at each other, and the
skinny little driver moaned hopeless epithets. He hunched
down behind the wheel, and kept his engine going in 'high
and in gear, longing to take off, but plainly more compassionate to us as fellow victims of Society after one look at the
rusty little freighter.

Cranes were hoisting big crates and trunks, mostly wicker,
toward the two open hatches. We stared, because three of
them were ours, and it was baffling to see them swing up and
over the hatch and then come down ponderously again to
the dock. The police looked wildly at colored papers, and the
driver became more and more nervous, and gunned his motor
hysterically. He was frantic, but was too decent to dump us
there with all our bundles and packages and the accordion.
Probably, we felt, he had left his brood of small rat-faces
and some half-sloshed buddies to do this crazy favor for a
brother-in-law. . . .

Finally my husband talked to one of the excited police,
who laughed shortly when asked if the ship would sail that
day, and said in a cryptic manner that he would guarantee
it, but without some of its cargo. We could wait right there
on the dock, he said in a mocking way, and watch the fun.

Our driver, who looked more and more like a trapped
animal wanting to be anywhere on earth but there, helped
us feverishly to unload all the foolish packages of books
and cigarettes and toothpaste for a month's chancy living,

and shot off down the nearest alley without even a look at the money we had paid him.

His fraternal hopes for a better world had apparently not extended to the police, and neither, during the rest of the afternoon, did ours, as we stood in the thick air and watched a crew of uniformed men run long steel needles into every bundle and through every wicker crate and trunk on the dock. There was something doggedly vicious about it, and as the sweet fire of the Sicard liquor dimmed and vanished, we felt like three shocked ghosts, expelled from Heaven to an unknown level in Limbo; atonement in reverse. We were lost souls, wracked with puzzlements and vague horrors.

When the searchers got to our trunks and plunged their lethal wands through the woven sides, they hit something hard in one, and gathered around it, yelling and stabbing futilely. A pale ship's officer ran down the gangplank, looking wild and Italian. He talked for a minute with the police and then hurried toward us, calling out our names. Automatically we had our passports and tickets ready, and he apologized in a hysterical staccato and asked only if we had the trunk keys with us.

"Why?" my husband asked in a cold way I had never heard before but knew was based on the last fumes from Cassis. "That trunk contains scholastic material."

"And all our winter shoes," I added.

The young man cried impatiently, "The keys, please! Every ship in Marseille is being searched, sir. Three of the most dangerous murderers in the history of this decadent country are trying to escape to America, haven of criminals! They are perhaps on our vessel, because it is May Day and the criminal elements of this depraved Communistic serpents' nest are aiding them. They are typical Marseille toughs, pimps, murderers, arsonists, drug traffickers. So the *keys*! We are five hours late in sailing, for God's sake!"

He ran back madly to the police, brandishing our keys as if he had just won some kind of polemical battle at least. The uniformed men still kept trying to plunge their hideous needles at every angle in the book trunk. My husband moaned that his papers would be ruined forever. My sister Norah, as sardonic at fourteen as she is now, said grimly, "No blood, no murder, dummies." I said, "Dog eat dog." We felt old and sad.

The suspicious trunk flew open, and the books and the shoes were indeed in a sorry state, and the policemen hurried off the dock without more than a cursory salute to the ship's officer. They were the first and I think the last truly rude people I ever met in Marseille, on or off duty, if of course one accepts and forgives certain stresses of an occupational nature. Or perhaps it was those slim wands that prejudiced me. . . .

"This has been a nightmare, a catastrophe," the sweating officer told us in a belated bid for our numbed sympathy. "The ship has been invaded since noon, while every inch was searched. Then all the passengers' and officers' baggage had to be taken off. Never dock at Marseille," he suddenly shouted. "Never, ever! But especially on May Day! It is a pesthole. It is anti-Christ. The dinner gong will be in ten minutes, one hour and fifty-two minutes late!"

He dashed up the gangplank, leaving us silent on the dock, three people thinking of dappled sunlight on the balcony above the quiet Vieux Port, and the good meal, the wines slowly drunk, the potent liqueur and the nice proprietor. I should have offered to play him a little tune, I thought, once the clients had cleared out. Mostly, though, we thought about how sharp and fast those police needles were, thrusting thirstily into the bowels of every basket, looking for the bowels of every hidden wretch.

Once we were on board the miserable little hulk, our feelings about the ex-brigands who scuttled over it to keep us more or less fed and bedded for the next thirty-six days were more mixed than they might have been: had these wild-eyed human wrecks plotted to harbor three desperate fellow travellers along with us innocents heading toward the Land of the Free? We ate at the one mess table with the officers, and grew easy enough with them, but no word was ever said about our delayed sailing. Well after we landed in Paydro, though, we learned that according to the newspapers one of a suspected three Sicilian gangsters had indeed tried to join our ship in Marseille. He was hidden in a wicker trunk, which was carried into a small shed on the dock; some thirty bullets were jammed into it while our driver kept the cab's motor roaring and all the cops shouted louder than ever, to drown the unequivocal sounds.

I have travelled knowingly with many people in flight from one thing and another, and probably with many more I have not recognized. Of all of them, I feel sorriest for the man hopelessly folded into an airy creaking box, trying to get onto that filthy little ship on May Day. What difference could it have made to justice, to Marseille, to the total criminal population anywhere, if he had been able to emerge, once past Gibraltar, and then vanish through the Pacific Coast port authorities toward Chicago?

Years later I told my mother about this strange departure, and she said that once in about 1902 she was on a night train in Eastern Europe, and border police burst into her sleeping compartment with their swords drawn, and thrust them in a wide flash under both the berths, under the mattresses on which she and her companion lay, then into the racks above, where ladies in those days put their hats and such like. It happened in less than a minute, without a word said, and it was a breathless unforgettable adventure. Ours was actually more tedious. . . .

At home, there was the parcel of Paris-jazz-hot records we had left tipsily at the Mont Ventoux, with a scribble from the boss inviting us to come soon again. We did, but too late: he had vanished, although his restaurant still exists. And there are no more wicker trunks: the Gypsies have stopped making them, to the sorrow of provincial theatre troupes and impoverished students. They are fine for storing blankets, as well as for hiding a man or killing him invisibly, once neatly packed inside.

Chapter 11

THE GOOD OLD
BEAUVAU

I

The little street called Beauvau, for the prince who was governor of Provence in 1782, is the first to the right as one goes up the Canebière from the Vieux Port, and it ends three short blocks later at the Place de l'Opéra. By now it is a narrow subtly nervous place, disliked by drivers of anything on wheels, but in 1785 when the old quarter of the Arsenal of Galleys was rebuilt, it was an elegant but impressive thoroughfare with a fine perspective toward the beautiful theatre, and with the first real sidewalks in Marseille, made of bricks and with occasional stone posts to warn horsemen to stay where they belonged, in the unpaved roadway.

One of the first buildings on the new street housed the offices of the Post Master M. Barrochin, and the diligences stopped there, so that travellers could ask for mail that might have come on ahead. Stendhal was one of them, in

1805, when he came to Marseille to study with a famous local actress for his future book on love.

The Post Master moved, and by the time George Sand stayed there in 1839, the fine building had become a reputable and even stylish hotel, well known to travellers because of its cleanliness and its nearness to the Port. The Hotel Beauvau was a double refuge for Sand, who moved there from a hotel farther from the stench of the harbor, because the Marseillais were making plain to her their disapproval of her living openly with her lover Frédéric Chopin and her two children. (She had been once before in the town, six years earlier, with Alfred de Musset. . . .) She hated the town, full of smells and snubs, but stood it because Chopin was desperately ill and there was a famous lung specialist in the town who was somewhat scornfully rumored to be as attentive to the writer as he was to the musician. His skills did not succeed in getting George Sand into Marseille society, but Chopin revived enough to give an organ concert at Notre Dame, for a famous singer's funeral.

Another guest at the Hotel Beauvau was the poet Lamartine, who stayed there in 1832 before he set sail for the Orient. In spite of an open lack of enthusiasm among the townspeople for romantic effusions, a solemn reception was given for him, at which he read a lengthy, mellifluous ode to Marseille. In it he promised to return, which he did several times, accompanied once by his wife, and oftener by other ladies. And Prosper Mérimée stayed at the Good Old Beauvau in 1839, before embarking for Corsica. . . .

And my family and my friends and I have been staying there since our first magical lunch in its little restaurant in 1932. Since that May Day, when we too had to embark for Panama and California, knowing in bones and heart that we would return, the hotel has felt curiously like home. We seldom talk much about it to anyone who might hate it, as Mme. Sand did, but for different reasons. (The Port smells fine by now; Marseille society is fortunately not essential to us; compared with the ailing and exhausted travellers of the last century, we are eminently free from wanting or needing handsome medicos nearby. . . .)

The place has had sharp ups and downs in the past one hundred and fifty years, like most of us, and although it is currently immaculate and even somewhat elegant, I never suggest that people stay there without being certain-sure that they are right for it. For one thing, it could, like many another monument of seeming impregnability, become in seven days a shoddy dump, overrun by rats both two- and four-legged. For another, it is very noisy, if one stays on the water side, looking out over the whole exciting Old Port and down onto the long Quai des Belges, ugly in 1976 with upheavals for the new Métro, but soon (What is soon in that ancient place? A year? A century?) to be grassy and almost prim again, with at each end a familiar bronze child, piping and dancing. Yes, even on the top floor of the Beauvau, the noise is not for finicky ears. It lasts most of each twenty-four hours, what with ambulances and paddy wagons screaming in the night, and the small putt-putt of fishing boats before dawn. . . . Another (and perhaps the main) reason I am careful about suggesting that people go to the Beauvau, no matter how much I love them, is that it is where it is, in the heart of one of the greatest and therefore most wicked ports in the world.

The first time I ever did more than eat in the hotel I was with a fine old lady from Delaware who was discreetly terrified by this plain fact. At first I thought her unresponsive chilliness toward everything we did or ate was connected with the foreign drinking water, one of those touristic hazards never mentioned but deeply respected by people of her generation. Then I realized that in spite of the air of gentility then evident in the hotel, she was acutely miserable. A maid turned down her bed and pulled the heavy velvet curtains over the noise, the beautiful view. But then my normally dignified old friend put a chair under the window handles in case some thug lurked outside on her fifth-floor balcony, and she overlapped the thick curtains with safety pins as high. as she could reach, to foil Peeping Toms. She did not eat, being afraid of Mediterranean fish and repelled by both garlic and olive oil. We walked only on the Canebière, where the sidewalks were wide enough to eliminate pickpockets and jostlers. And of course we moved by the second night to a proper Anglo-American hotel near the St. Charles railroad station where, within a few hours, we took the first fast train to Cannes. It was a good lesson for me, in my study of People-and-Places.

I ignore most of the rules when I feel that the gamble may be worth it, but I have half-lost the throw a few times, and occasionally think I should quit my far-from-academic playing. Once, about ten years after the Liberation, I invited an old family counselor to stay at the Beauvau with us. We were used to very shabby furnishings in post-war Aix, and although we knew that the Good Old Beauvau had not been decently refurbished since it was used by the Occupiers during the Occupation, we were never aware of the stained carpets with holes in them, the faded dingy curtains with a few rings rattling loose on the bent rods, the cracked tiles in the 1910 bathrooms, until we saw the shock and patient disapproval of our dear friend.

He found a good chair with its springs intact, and spent most of his days there sitting with his back to the Vieux Port, reading London and New York papers and occasionally pulling out long green silk threads from the tattered upholstery. He left the hotel room only to go to luncheon and dinner, and fortunately there were some excellent restaurants to which, also fortunately, because he believed Marseille too dangerous a city to walk in, there were available taxis. When we were going less than two blocks from the Beauvau, I murmured to the driver to circulate for ten minutes . . . and although our friend spoke excellent French, he was apparently too apprehensive to pay attention to what was said to the cutthroat at the wheel. (There was also a dark corridor on the second floor, which led directly to the corner restaurant, and which I used for rainy nights and often found useful for visitors like our otherwise fearless old lawyer.)

Another time, in 1973, I ignored my unwritten game-rules too carelessly, and literally scared off our lifelong friends from Britain. As I have said, they came for a week with my sister Norah and me in Marseille and left in three days, so fast we could hardly enjoy more than their dust. Everything went wrong while they were with us, in the hotel or out: windy weather; extra noise from one of the celebrations that roar beneficently through the old town every few weeks; a touch of gut trouble blamed on garlic or olive oil or else a broody oyster (it could not have been the local water, since they carefully primed all that with drams of bedroom Scotch . . .); a general feel of apprehension and uneasiness. But by 1975 or so, both Time and Space had smoothed their mysterious salves over all of us, and letters between California and Aberdeenshire recovered their old innocent affection.

Never again, though, will I gamble with the Good Old Beauvau as *pawn*. It is too precious to be tarnished, bruised, not in its own awareness but in mine.

At first there was a tall, boxlike piece of furniture to the left as one entered the lobby, with a stool in it. The Concierge sat there in front of his books, and registered guests and answered questions and supervised every come-and-go, every strange intruder, every honored resident, as if we were unruly children in the cloister of a strict convent school. We tiptoed. People who sat across the elegant shabby lobby from him, behind the imposing vase of fresh flowers that was always there, whispered or stayed silent, and tried not to rattle their papers.

The Concierge was a tall, boxlike piece of furniture, too. He had one of the most disapproving, sneering, dour faces I ever saw, and his taciturn coldness could make me shake with frustration and almost weep, but in some forty years I came to think of him not only as honest and dedicated to his profession, but as a human being who knew and remembered me over long blank periods and who approved as warmly as he could permit himself of my children and even me.

Once I telephoned from Aix (a project in itself, involving over a half-hour of maneuverings in the nearest public booth, several blocks from our house), to ask him if he could get us tickets for the benefit vaudeville show at the Opera on Christmas Eve. He was icy with scorn and disapproval. Was I planning to expose my *children* to this exhibition of magic and lewdness? Should he ask for half-fare for the innocents? I was reduced to protesting that we had seen the show before, that it was like an English pantomime, that it was to help old vaudevillians. Why should I excuse myself? But I cringed before his grey sour face at the other end of the telephone, at the tall ornately carved desk in the Beauvau. "The children love it," I cried. "The tickets will be here when you arrive on Friday," he said curtly, and I stumbled out of the booth, ready to sob at such presumptuous hardness.

It was impossible to enter or leave the Beauvau without

passing his pulpit and his cold hateful stare, and I invented reasons to make him smile, but never succeeded. Will you please tell me when a good train leaves for Bologna? Is fresh cod in season now? Is the library at the Chamber of Commerce in the old Stock Exchange open on Mondays? He had every answer, in countless books around his legs, invisible to us circulating idiots who were not he, not the Concierge.

I came to think of him as unflinching, eternal, like Gibraltar but a little nicer. About thirty-five years after I met him, when the pulpit had been hauled away and he stood behind the Reception Desk, flanked by lissome young assistants in Pierre Cardin suits and backed by nearsighted kind girls at typewriters, I told him that I was snowbound in Marseille and that if I could not leave within three days for Paris I would be there for some time and flat broke. He shrugged disdainfully, with an impatient gesture, and said in a cold voice, "Please forget it. Stay as long as you want. We are not disquieted." Since "they" were not, neither was I.

Another time I invited an English family to stay a week at the hotel, while my sister and I lived out farther on the Vieux Port, and the morning I brought flowers for their room and their arrival, I told the Concierge that because the International Stock Exchange had closed that day, I might not be able to pay the bill until . . . "Please," he said disagreeably. "Do not discuss it further. We know you." I said no more.

Once he *almost* smiled, when I asked him if he could recommend some places around the Vieux Port for a few months of residence. He pulled out a real-estate list and crossed off at least twenty places with a murmured description of strangely lurid pastimes available in each. He made a neat list of two. "These may possibly be suitable," he said, and as I left the lobby I knew he was watching me with overt pity but perhaps, *perhaps* a tinge of warmth.

When my sister and I got the apartment we had always had in our subconscious wishes, we bought a big bunch of Transvaal daisies at the Flower Market, and left them at the old Beauvau. It was the Concierge's day off, but later one of the nice girls in glasses said he wished us to be thanked for our courteous attention. He himself never mentioned the silly posy, in several more meetings, and stayed as icy as ever, in spite of his almost familial involvement in our various lives.

I do not know his name; he has always been referred to as He, or *M. le Concierge*. By 1976 he had retired, I was told. If he is still alive, I am sure he is as nasty as ever, and I know I like him, and miss his sour gloom in the lobby.

There is one other person I miss there, who left when the Concierge did: a dark-browed man with cowlike eyes. He was the size of a midget, but heavy-shouldered, and he carried suitcases from the sidewalk to the rooms, up, down, out, in. He grew bald while we knew him, and spoke with the fruitiest Provençal accent I ever heard. The last time I saw him, squeezed into the two-person elevator with several bags and me, he asked very shyly if I remembered him, and then, "How are the little girls?" I told him they had children of their own. He looked unbelieving, but said nothing until he left me in my room, when he muttered something almost unintelligible about how Time passes, eh, Madame? He had tears in his dumb brown eyes, and ran out the door.

Now dapper, frail boys stagger under the airplane luggage, and elegantly dressed and coiffed oldsters of perhaps twenty-three man Reception, still backed by nearsighted typists and telephone girls. The flowers are gone from the little cluster of tables and chairs in the lobby, and if one doesn't know of a delightful low sitting room between the ground floor and the next official one, where flowers always bloom for the aficionados of the Good Old Beauvau, the place looks un-inviting, even without the Concierge.

At the time he sneered down on us all from his high pulpit, there were curved glass cases on the lobby walls, to display perfumes and scarves and other touristic fancies. Gradually they emptied and grew haphazard, if not openly neglected: a few rolls of Kodak film, two flyspecked *santons*, a hand-painted scarf saying "Souvenir du Château d'If." Since about 1971 they have been taken down, to nobody's chagrin.

But until about then, there was a direct path, indicated by deliberately unreadable signs, up strange stairs and down corridors, to the hotel restaurant. The route was dank and smelly. One went past the kitchens, sure of being lost or unwelcome, and suddenly there was a lovely room, glass on two sides, sparkling with silver and goblets and stiff linens. It never seemed anything but good to me, although of course I had eaten meals there that my friends did not find as special as I. The service was not only excellent but *concerned*, so that it seemed to matter to everyone if the salad dressing was correct, or the orange tart crisp. This temple of welcome has gone, like the Concierge and the midget porter and countless other permanencies. But it may rise again, and I hope it will once more have a secret upstairs tunnel from the hotel, for rainy nights and wary strangers.

Meanwhile, outside the hotel door on the Rue Beauvau, is a small well-incised plaque, high enough above the sidewalk to stay free of graffiti:

> Alphonse de Lamartine en 1832
> Frédéric Chopin   en 1839
> George Sand
> séjournèrent en cet hôtel

and I smile at the sight and the thought of it, because underneath, there is another smaller notice, invisible of course
except to a chosen few:

We too, in 1932 and on—

I I

By now I have spent all four seasons of the year on or near
the Vieux Port, although it has taken me a long time to do it.
I know the look and smell of the place at its best and perhaps
its worst, as far as wind and weather can go, and of course
I have been very uncomfortable there. Once in late July
I looked up the Canebière and wondered if I could walk to
the next bit of awning shade without falling down in the
white-hot glare. Once I thought my hour had come, in a small
boat trying to return from the New Port, La Joliette, around
the small stretch of open wild tossing Mediterranean into the
Old Port. And of course there have been times of whims and
megrims . . . stars and planets pulling all of us this way and
that, willy-nilly, tidal waves in small ponds and teapots. But
what remains is good. It always has been. And the old hotel
on the Quai des Belges has mysteriously been its core.

It seems strange that I have spent several Christmases in
Marseille. They are like glass-headed pins on a map, fixing
Time into a conditioned focus: it is clearer to think of December 25 than of March 22, or even July 4, I suppose, in any
given year of a lifetime.

It may be even stranger that several of those holidays on
my inner calendar were located in the Good Old Beauvau,
as many other times have been. Again one wonders what pin
holds hard to the physical and spiritual map a certain locality.
Why that place? But that place it was, without argument.

One of the times, when I was living in Aix in the 1950s
with my little girls, we went with instinctive directness to the
Beauvau, and what happened there made me remember a
jingle I once knew, by Thackeray, I think:

> Christmas is here:
> Winds whistle shrill,
> Icy and chill.
> Little care we;
> Little we fear
> Weather without,
> Sheltered about
> The Mahogany Tree.

I dreaded for the children the sudden awareness of being in
a far country that can engulf Occidental travellers at Christmas more probably than any other time. If I had never actually felt it myself, I knew it lurked like a sad sickness, an
almost invisible malaise, for many people. I reflected often, as
the season approached, about what best to do to keep my girls
happy and warm and gay when they would be light-miles
from everything they had always known at home.

Friends were kind to us, in the face of the truism that
Noël to Frenchmen means doors locked against the world,
tight family ritual. I refused their solicitude and made one
of those arbitrary, almost brutal decisions familiar to guardi-
ans and other duly appointed dictators, and on December 24
we took the bus into Marseille, to the edge of the Old Port
and the small hotel we knew happily, from other such private
flights—the Good Old Beauvau.

There is nothing much grimmer, I have heard too often,
than Christmas in a hotel bedroom. I felt quite free from
bravado, but I was bent upon disproving this for the three
of us, somewhat as if staring the obvious in the eye would be

more of a real diversion than peering obliquely at it from the friendly courtesies of Madame Lanes or the Aubergy family. We were thousands of miles from home, in a shabby old building in a dubious port-town . . . and we reacted to my deliberate dare like healthy firehorses at the sound of the bell: never had I seen my girls more sparkling and alive, nor myself felt surer.

The two rooms were familiar to us. First thing, we pulled back the once-elegant curtains as usual, to see all we could of the Quai below, and the Vieux Port, packed with fishing boats and a few big yachts docked for the winter and one American Navy craft, nosed in right at our feet, by the stone that marks where the first sailors may have landed more than two thousand years ago.

When Anne and Mary asked where we were going to open the secrets that we had all been wrapping furtively in Aix for Christmas morning, I suddenly knew what had been bothering my subconscious. "We'll grow a tree for them," I said. "Oh, of course," the children said. And there in front of the tall bright windows, as if a magic seed had been planted in the stained old carpet, grew the hatrack from the little hallway.

It was even taller than I, made of Victorian mahogany, shaped into a slender trunk, a sudden curling of branches at the top like a wildly functional palm tree, for gentlemen's hats and coats, with at the bottom convenient shorter curls to put our secret bundles in. It was perfect.

We left it there in the light, an earnest for the future, bare but ready.

Outside the air was cold and exciting. People rushed this way and that, clutching parcels and scarves and hats, gathering in knots and then melting back, around old men playing trick instruments that sounded now like guitars and now

horns or drums, and two women with a troupe of trained
mice shivering in the wind, and a fat man lying on a worn
rug, while a boy, paper-thin, did somersaults and pirouettes
on the upstretched massive feet. . . .

First we went along the edge of the Old Port to the ferry
crossing, a part of our Marseille pattern, like pulling back
the curtains. If we had ever felt in danger in that tiny harbor,
we knew we were safe on Christmas Eve, for in the middle
of the stuffy little flat boat was a crèche, shivering gently to
the pound of the engine below it.

There was a Holy Family, perhaps two inches high, with
the Baby Jesus in his cradle, and there were the shepherds,
and even three tiny sheep following the Wise Men. The
santons were everywhere in Provence at Christmastime in
those far days, and Anne and Mary approved happily and
pointed out characters they already knew from the dozens of
them in *La Pastorale*, a version of the Nativity, as much of
the Midi as garlic and *pastis*. Before the five-minute voyage
ended with a good bump against the opposite quay, we had
each added some coins to the conveniently large shell by the
Manger, for the crew of our doughty little ship. . . .

We passed judgment on a few more crèches that afternoon,
in spite of our hurry: a favorite bar, a good restaurant, stores,
bank windows. The *santons* were usually bigger, often more
beautiful, dressed in rich silks and jewels sometimes, but we
liked best the tiny figures standing in sand and seaweed on
the ferryboat.

The crowds grew denser as the light greyed. There was still
much we must do, to make the Mahogany Tree thrive, and
I felt that I should keep everything more than life-size, however I dared, to hold us firmly in Marseille, not drifting
toward California.

That is why I let the little girls go off alone, for the first time in that town, with some money and some directions. "Buy shiny little bonbons," I said nonchalantly. "And stay on the Canebière. And don't go up it more than three blocks. And always cross with a lot of other people. And come straight back to the hotel." And I hurried away from them, not daring to look past the sight of Mary's hand in Anne's. My heart lurched. I felt one flash of horror at what I had done, to send my children alone into the jungle.

When I dashed into the lobby with a bag from the pastry shop, and two bundles of Christmas Roses I had bought from a streetseller, and some caviar and champagne and a ball of red string, Anne and Mary sat primly behind the high carved desk of the Concierge, like two small trunks to be delivered to our rooms. Their laps were piled with many more paper bags and packages than I had given them money for.

Upstairs, we went through their loot. Storekeepers had insisted, they told me solemnly, that they take a few samples of things along with what they actually bought: pipe cleaners to make into strange shapes, a bag of gold-covered chocolate coins to hang from the wooden branches, handfuls of brightly wrapped bonbons, a surprising mesh bag filled with little plastic airplanes and tanks and racing cars, "half-price to us because we are so far from home," I was told blandly.

Anne invented a way to coil red string up the tree trunk and hang things from it. Mary fitted our secret packages around the bottom. I did the tall work. All the time, below us and out to the Fort St. Nicolas, the Old Port lay black and heaving, covered with boats glinting in the lights from the bright quays, the two dogged little ferries crisscrossing, and cars and buses blowing their whistles into the crowds of heedless excited people, and above everything, perhaps more sacred than profanely pagan, the steady golden radiance of the great statue of Notre Dame de la Garde, to guide us to safety from the farthest wave.

Our tree was beautiful, too. We turned off the lights, and let the Vieux Port glow behind it. The little candies and toys swung slowly on their long strings from the topknot of branches, and beneath them the Christmas secrets waited.

We ate a small slow meal in a little restaurant where the family *santons*, carved from olivewood and dressed in ancient woven costumes, made one more crèche for us, and the cook, already gently illuminated by his own Christmas spirits, sang the children a long Provençal carol about the shepherds watching their flocks by night. Back at the Beauvau, Mary took a nap, and Anne and I sat silently in a big chair by our Mahogany Tree, watching the Port. While we were at dinner the Navy craft had turned on long strings of flickering colored lights, and lanterns moved slowly up and down on the small boats in the windy night, and all the cafés along the Quai du Port and the fishhouses of the Rive Neuve were bright . . .

. . . and suddenly the bells were ringing everywhere . . .

. . . and we pushed coat and mittens onto Mary, and ran out into the town again. We were late: it was just midnight. We moved with other laughing, hurrying people along the Quai des Belges toward the old church that is sinking back into the marshes of the Lacydon. Inside, we could not go faster than inches toward where we knew the altar was. We heard the faint chanting of the Mass. Even so far back, the air was shimmering from all the candles, and smelled of incense and beeswax, garlic and holiday libations. The organ thundered wheezily over our heads in the choirloft, and boys sang like birds, and more people surged in against us from the windy street.

I held onto my girls, invisible in the mass of heavily wrapped, panting, shoving Marseillais, and then as well as I could I worked us back to the big door and *out*. We stood for a moment, getting used to the secular air. I bought candles from a piteous woman on the steps. Mary, still half asleep, asked sadly why she had not been there when the new Baby Jesus was born, and I gave her the candles as promise that we would come back early in the morning to find Him there.

At home, our tree gleamed for us in the light from below, and its richly colored fruits glinted in the air we had set moving. Ah, it is beautiful, we agreed, and went straight into sleep, instead of sitting up wickedly, gaily, as we had long planned, carousing gently in the French custom for Noël.

Before daybreak, the bells burst into their Christmas song again, all over town, a thousand different exultant tones, always with the grave sound of Notre Dame de la Garde dominating. We hurried toward the church with our candles, and the nave, almost empty, was still filled with the glowing light from all the pyramids of them blazing and burning. We went slowly up to the crêche beside the great altar, where life-size *santons* stood regally or knelt with awe before the manger . . . but there, to Mary's repressed astonishment, mixed with deep dismay, were *two* cradles, with a Baby Jesus in each one! She behaved like a true Christian, ready to accept any miracle at its appointed moment, but later explanations and native logic did little to allay her basic confusion, and even Time has not quite wiped out that first chagrin. Her child's faith doubtless suffered more than my wearier acceptance could. But even I felt a clinical distaste for the newer of the two Babes.

The first was the "right" one: a faded, scratched doll of papier-mâché and wax, grossly fat like all such images of two hundred years ago, to denote well-being and contentment.

It was dressed in yellowed linen trimmed sparingly with crude lace, and one finger was gone from its pudgy raised pink hand. It lay on real straw, and around the old cradle, which looked as if it had rocked many human babies, were bowls of green and black olives, some loaves of fresh bread, a few bottles of wine, and one small cheese on a cotton napkin.

The other Christ Child lay on an ornate rayon pillow in its polished crib, so that no lowly straw might show, and it was a modern doll with luxuriant blond curls, and a ruffled christening robe intertwined with ribbons and frothing with nylon lace. Its half-closed eyes were languorous behind long lashes, and its mouth was pursed over white even teeth, ready to say *Maman.* I cannot remember that any gifts had been brought to it.

We lit candles here and there in the echoing church, and then gave coins to the piteous vendor still dozing outside, waved to a familiar bus driver at the Aix-stop on the Quai, and hurried home to our tree, with all the bells still pealing.

The sun was up. The ripe fruits twinkled and twirled on their long stems. We flipped our beds into shape, pushed a little table next to the Tree, telephoned for pots of hot milk and coffee and extra plates. I brought in last night's untouched feast from the balcony.

There was a new young waiter, whose lonesome face lit up when he saw our celebration. We picked some of our fruit for him, and he took a few sips of champagne and went off almost gaily, with tacit approval.

Then we ate one of the strangest Christmas breakfasts of our combined lives: caviar on hot rolls, big cups of frothy café au lait for Anne and Mary and the cool dry wine for me, and finally, thick ceremonious slices, so far past our slaked hunger that they became pure sensuality, from the *Bûche de Noël* I had bought. It was the smallest Christmas

Log in all Marseille, probably, but even so its rich chocolate bark, its inner trunk of whipped cream and delicate dark sponge cake, its leaves from the dainty sprigs of holly shaped in almond paste, almost made us reel in our chairs. We sat back like Roman banqueters, stunned, waiting half comatose in the bright sunlight for digestion to rescue us.

Anne suddenly produced three tiny bottles made of chocolate wrapped in silver foil. They were, she assured me unblinkingly, filled with a nonalcoholic digestive, highly recommended to her by a charming man in a wine shop she had dropped into during her Christmas marketing. Mary added firmly, as a future medico of the family, that they were indeed indicated for just such an emergency as our present one, and that they had not cost a sou, because of the seasonal jollity. . . . Pure flim-flam, I decided with some maternal satisfaction, and smiled at my innocents.

We bit off the chocolate corks of the dwarf-size potions, and solemnly toasted each other and California and the world in general, with some drops of what may well have been a digestive, and gradually we revived, and the shabby old bedroom took on its final triumphant look of Christmas, with drifts of tissue paper from our secret packages piled on the stained red carpet. The air hummed with cries and murmurs of pleasure, above the sound of all Marseille hurrying to late Mass, early lunch at Aunt Mary-Martha's, a holiday *pastis* at Mario's Bar-Grill. Below our windows the Old Port lifted and fell gently after yesterday's small wind. Over it all, us, the Port, the whole wonderful old town, rose our Mahogany Tree, hanging rich and generous with its harvest of bright fruits.

I thought of singing. Then I remembered how far away we might still feel from home. I began to tell Anne and Mary about Old Joseph of Arimethaea, and of how he wandered far from Jerusalem, perhaps with a Holy Grail under his arm. When he got to Glastonbury in England, I told them as we sat under our Tree, he stuck his dry hawthorn staff into the ground, and it burst into leaves and blossoms to celebrate Christ's birth. Twigs from that staff still bloom, at Christmastime . . . just as we knew that other dead stalks in other lands east, south, west, north, could bring forth their own blossoms and sweet berries, and for the same reasons.

We felt safe and trusting—*home.*

A CONCLUSION

Yes.

Like Mme. de Sévigné, I am giddied by "the whole atmos-
phere . . . the sea, the fortresses, the mountains. . . ." And
I would *be* there, past, present, future. I would be near the
Vieux Port, within sight and feel of it.

One day I found the Harbor Master. It took me some time,
partly because I did not know his correct title of Port Captain.
I asked at the big Criée on the Rive Neuve, and was referred
to a couple of small cafés and a chandlery.

The cafés were the kind that fell silent when I went in,
first because I was a female foreigner who obviously did not
know where she was, and second because I asked a question
the people preferred not to answer: Where was the Harbor
Master? (Later I learned from him that the owners and
workers at the public fish auctions were at odds with him,
choosing to stay right where they were on the Rive Neuve
when he wanted to move them up the coast.) The chandlery

was run, hopefully for a short time, by a bewildered beautiful young drifter from Rouen or someplace far north, and he fluttered helplessly and then suggested I go across the street to the most important of the yacht clubs, which I did.

It was covered with signs warning me not to set foot in it, but I went up the elegant gangplank and read a dramatic map of the moorings available to the members and a delicious menu for that night's dinner, before I was ushered in and then out of a busy little man's office: he could do nothing for me and knew nothing at all about anything I hoped to learn. (Later I suspected that he too preferred not to recall the Harbor Master, whose proletarian opinion that the valuable privately controlled moorings along the quays really belonged to the city of Marseille, for fair taxation anyway, was unpalatable.)

I went off the Rive Neuve, up to the Rue Sainte, which used to be the road that led Greeks and then Romans to their cemeteries high on the hill where St. Victor was later built. On one of the old buildings I found a grimy brass plate saying something like Reunion Society of Pleasure Boat-Owners, and went into a dark smelly hallway and halfway up the first flight of some rotting narrow stairs before I heard myself telling me to turn around and leave, get out, forget the reason for being in such a foul sinister deserted building. Victorian words like *malodorous, invidious*, were in my head, and when I got back onto the Rue Sainte, I felt a childish relief that nobody had heard my steps or run after me, scrabbling ratlike . . . twisted little legs . . . one ear under a straggle of grey hair . . . "Madame, Madame! Come back! Come smile at me. . . ."

I walked firmly down to the Rive Neuve again, and banged on a couple of locked doors in the bright sunlight, small neat clubhouses for the Bargemen's Union, the Jolly Syndicate of

Oars and Anchors. Finally a man in the bait shack at the bend of the Rive Neuve into the Quai des Belges sent me, correctly enough, to Number Three on the Quai du Port.

It was easy, too easy after my various frustrations, right off the far end of the Quai opposite the little bait shop, and I felt encouraged. But Number Three was a small souvenir store run by an attractive plump woman who explained compassionately to me that the Quai du Port *naturally* started at both ends and stopped at the Town Hall in the middle, or something like that. I would find the Harbor Master at Number Three at the other end, she said.

The day was hot and by then I was footweary and there was tomorrow, so I waited for it behind a cool glass of rosé. And in some twenty hours I was at the sea end of the Quai, a place familiar to me for many years because of the fine small buildings there, which I never even dreamed were occupied by the elusive Captain and his crew. I felt shy about simply walking through the gate by the first of the two matching Italianate pavilions and asking to see the boss, but there had been no apparent way to telephone for an appointment. I pretended I was a young, eager, beautiful girl-reporter in a TV serial. . . .

The buildings are lovely, especially from across the Port: low, graceful. The first was built in 1719, to house the officials of the Health and Sanitation works, and its twin sister was added in the nineteenth century. There is a famous statue of St. Roch over the gateway, erected to protect Marseille against the Plague, "Scourge of Provence." It is perhaps more a symbol of blind faith than of terror by now, but well repaired after an American corvette knocked it down while maneuvering up to the Quai for a medical inspection in 1839. There used to be important carvings and paintings inside, mostly about health and sanitation, of course (i.e., disease and sewage . . .), but they have been moved to better housing, and by 1973 when I went to meet the Harbor Master, the large light rooms were sparsely furnished, very clean, with a few bright posters and blown-up photographs of the Vieux Port on their walls, and the tall graceful windows wide open. (In 1976 all the business was located on a large square floating dock, while the fine old pavilions underwent restoration as valuable historical architecture.)

At first I thought nobody worked there. It was as quiet as a country garden-house. Then a lone young man spotted my obvious confusion about where to find the Captain behind one of the unmarked open doors, and when I told him why I was there he conferred somewhere. The hall I was in was bare and airy, and a bee buzzed in and then out onto the waterfront. I could hear a typewriter somewhere, tapped hesitantly. The clerk beckoned to me, and I went into a big, almost naked office where he introduced me to Captain Agostelli and then left.

The Harbor Master was a tall, square man, more like a Northerner than a Marseillais except for his dark eyes. He was courteous in a gruff way, and reminded me of Inspector Maigret, which I finally told him. That seemed to please him very much. I soon stopped trying to be a bright, scared newshen and felt like myself, always comfortable with an attractive person across from me.

Captain Agostelli was talkative, in the easy way of a man who has nothing in the world to do but chat about his main interest in life. It seemed impossible that he watched over the whole Port, like an eagle, like a beagle, like Maigret himself, as we sat there in the fresh salty air and he told me of what was happening that day, that minute, outside the window.

In April of 1973, the Captain estimated, there were about

2,600 boats of all categories there: 1,696 pleasure craft, mostly sail; 250 motorcraft in the small marinas of the Lacydon off the Rive Neuve; 372 fishing boats, of which 115 were more than 12 meters long; 373 yachts in passage of ten days or less. Of these last, 163 were French, 107 English, 18 American, 27 Panamanian (American), 22 Belgian, 8 Dutch, 7 German and 7 Spanish, 5 Italian, and the rest Austrian, Portuguese, Bermudan, Canadian, Argentinian, Puerto Rican, and so on.

Most of the yachts, he said, were very rich, into port for fuel on their way to more stylish moorings, where their owners would meet them by plane. Their crews were highly skilled in every possible way, he said noncommittally.

On all the trawlers in port, the *chalutiers*, of more than twelve meters and often with deep draft, there was a large floating population of foreign fishermen, with two or three Frenchmen as owner-captains. Their papers were kept firmly in order, and for a stay of more than one or two days, the crewmen had to report with their *permis de séjour* to the Marseille Police Headquarters. The men were mostly Portuguese in 1973, with Arabs next, and then a scattering of every other nation, and all of them wanted to bring their families to Marseille.

The low-cost housing problem, Captain Agostelli said, was tight for these people. Local fishermen made as many as a couple of short sorties a day, but the trawlers often went out for three or more, for tuna, and sometimes for several weeks. The women and children needed decent quarters, and HLM was obviously the answer to the worldwide and age-old question, Who will pay? (HLM, which in French sounds like an exotic Moslem word, Ash-el-Emm, is often mentioned in Provence and probably everywhere in France, and stands for *Habitations à Loyer Modéré*. . . .) Of course the families wanted to be near the Port, not out in the suburbs. This meant demolition, high-rise, more non-French. . . . He shrugged hopelessly.

Another current problem was the relocation of the public fish auctions, the big Criée and the two or three smaller ones. They were destined to be moved from the Rive Neuve to a new port designed especially for the collection and distribution of the catch, at Somaty, between the big harbor of La Joliette and l'Estaque, where Cézanne once painted. Everything was (and still is) ready: conveyor belts, proper loading zones for the fleets of trucks from all over Europe, a quick-freeze installation, railroad tracks. But the *criées* could not come to terms, to the exasperation of the Port authorities and especially of the Captain.

Still another thing that plainly made him fret and perhaps lose sleep was that nobody ever seemed to know who was responsible for harbor improvements. This had been going on for centuries, he growled. In 1784, for instance, when the lands belonging to the Grand Arsenal of Galleys were sold, a majestic plan to enlarge the Port was proposed. The government, of course, would have nothing to do with it. It seems that the Port had belonged to the city since the thirteenth century, and anyway it had never been made clear who owned the water itself and the quays. Furthermore, nobody was willing to claim possession of anything at all, because of the proposed expenses for improvement! And the citizens were pleased with things as they were; in spite of the infamous stench they had pleasant views, an agreeable promenade along the Quai du Port, a safe harbor for storm-bound vessels. . . .

I asked the Captain about the Chamber of Commerce. He

threw up his hands, and muttered that it was the same in those days as today: independent, implacable, impossible. Occasionally, as in 1838 when the town refused to widen the Quai du Port, the Chamber put up some 800,000 francs, mostly to thwart the Municipal Council by forcing it to let some of the nice old buildings be demolished. In the same finagling way, a new port for the dangerously flammable job of caulking ships was installed just under St. Victor on the Rive Neuve, with the city bowing out and the government taking charge and, of course, the Chamber of Commerce contributing 600,000 francs. . . .

"And now?" It was plain to me that the Captain was whipping a favorite nag.

"Now," he said almost ominously, "I must sit here and watch a slow rape of this fine old Port. In New York, where I worked with the Port Authority for more than a year, learning, learning, every inch dockside is privately owned and paid for. Therefore rents and taxes are completely controlled. Here in Marseille everything is now in the hands of the city, and supposedly the people, and is therefore corrupt and ill-managed."

I felt almost uneasy at his candid vehemence, for posters from the last elections were still peeling off the town walls, and I knew who owned the local newspapers and a little of what the town fathers were promising. He was indiscreet.

"Do you know the Société Nautique du Lacydon?" he asked, thumping his desk the way an impatient bull will paw the ground when nobody is looking. His face was red.

I told him that I looked down on it from where I lived above St. Victor: a neat small port filled with pleasure boats. He snorted. "That was an enormous job, all footed by the City of Marseille, with no repayment of any kind demanded for the first three years, and with memberships in what amounts to a rich private club selling for huge sums that go into the club itself! Who owns it? Is the city collecting any taxes? And who paid for it? It cost us millions, I tell you!"

He stood up and loosened his collar and sat down again. "I learned a lot in New York," he said mildly. "And what do you think of our sewage? This was once the foulest port in the Western world."

I told him that it smelled fairly clean to me . . . compared, for instance, to the East River around the docks in New York. Of course, I said cautiously, there were always bits of rubbish brushing against the Quai des Belges before the garbage-sweep sucked them up . . . especially after a holiday. . . .

He said, "There again! The government! The town! In 1837 several studies were made of how to swill out this bucket, after the City had organized a futile system of pontoons with scoops and so on, but the State declined to mix in what it called 'a local problem.' And here we are, known worldwide as the filthiest, most stinking port in the world! We had one little scow that went around, called *Marie-Salope*, Mary the Slut. By 1857 the Port was so filled with silt that even she could not navigate well, and the pollution was incredible. We were getting about 150 liters of filthy water a second, to flush out a Port with an overall water surface of some 27,000 square meters! Then in 1850 Longchamps brought us the clean water of the Durance, a steady flow of more than a thousand liters a second." He stood up again, tightened his tie, and said, "We still have *Marie-Salope* on duty. The open pipes are connected to a main one that dumps away from shore, and the household garbage is carted off to Le Crau, but . . . no doubt New York has its problems too."

"No doubt," I said. He sat down just before I stood up to

thank him and go. He looked strong and unruffled. "There is always something interesting going on here," he said chattily. "Perhaps you could help me with a little problem. . . ."

I could not keep from laughing, and it was then that I told him he reminded me very much of Simenon's Inspector Maigret. He looked enormously pleased, and almost smirked as he leaned back and said, "I should be puffing at a pipe! Well, the come-and-go of yachts here is really much too casual for my own comfort, and I have one sticky little situation on my hands right now that involves one of your countrymen. You know that when a skipper comes in, he shows me his passport, but no note is made of it here?"

"We have to in hotels," I interrupted, and he said, "Yes, but not in ports. It is careless, all right, but it's a French tradition. And an American with an odd name, something like Hirsh Guinafrom, from some little town in perhaps New Jersey, docked here about ten months ago, complete with a crew of one beautiful dame, and showed me a passport which I returned to him, and then he disappeared. He and the woman simply vanished.

"In about six months I began to get a lot of complaints from other boat owners about the dangerous condition of the abandoned yacht, and I wrote to the town in America. Answer: 'Person Unknown.' "

I felt as if I were reading the last book off the Presses de la Cité, with Maigret across the desk from me instead of his Marseille sibling. I suggested in a rather ambiguous way that the local American Consul would probably be able to verify the name and address if such a passport still existed, or even if it did not. The name did not sound quite right, I said.

Agostelli sighed as if he were tired, weary, exhausted. "Perhaps it will have to come to that," he muttered. But I could see that he much preferred to let the unwelcome deserted boat rot or burn or sink, or break loose and drift out to sea. . . .

We looked appreciatively at each other, he because I had told him he reminded me of a mutual hero, and I because he was a pleasant person, and after my thanks I left the bright, salty air of his office with regret. I was glad I had tracked him down.

On the way home, around the three sides of the Vieux Port, I felt at ease, perhaps more than ever before. There were things I missed: the jugglers at Christmastime in the fifties; my children then; the man I called Bacchus who for a while in the sixties sold shells marked "Coastal," "Local," "Exotic," while he looked peacefully at the Port and drank five or six liters a day of dark red wine; the strangest beggar of my whole life in the doorway of the old church sinking into the marshes of the Lacydon.

He was perhaps the last of the great army of professional mendicants who once almost ruled the town of Marseille, and occupied the Vieille Charité and directed the funerals and weddings of the helpless citizens with their threats and payments. He lay motionless and soundless, comatose, in rain and blazing heat, one leg cut off, hardly a living thing except for a small trickle of urine that now and then seeped out. Someone must have come at night to pile him onto a cart and take him away until the next morning, and dump a few coins out of the old mariner's cap that lay by him all day. It was hard to look at him, except as a once-man, until the day when I made myself see past his bloated face, past his one leg, past his thin red hair, and he opened his bright pale blue eyes and gazed straight at me, and I knew who he was.

Twenty years and fifteen years before, he had been the strong bold Gypsy-boy in Aix, a jaunty gimpy with a crutch and blazing hair, and red-haired, blue-eyed babies by every little skinny Gypsy-girl in town. He had swung boldly up and down the Cours Mirabeau, never begging, but watching his girl-women at their trades. I had seen him since he was perhaps fourteen, when he already had one small girl pregnant and proud.

He looked fully at me, and I at him, because he knew exactly who I was. I felt shaken. The recognition was ageless. Then his eyes closed, and he was a bag of rotted rags and bones, and I went down the quay past the bus stop to Aix, knowing that I had touched Time on the sleeve.

Perhaps that is what makes it essential that I be in Marseille, to stay in active contact with immortality now and then. It is not necessary to have a dead man look into my eyes, any more than it is to talk with a fine healthy Port Captain or watch my children skip carefully between the long nets laid out to be mended, tomorrow or twenty years ago. But how can I know, otherwise?